# The Creation of a University:
The Drury Story Continues
1977–2004

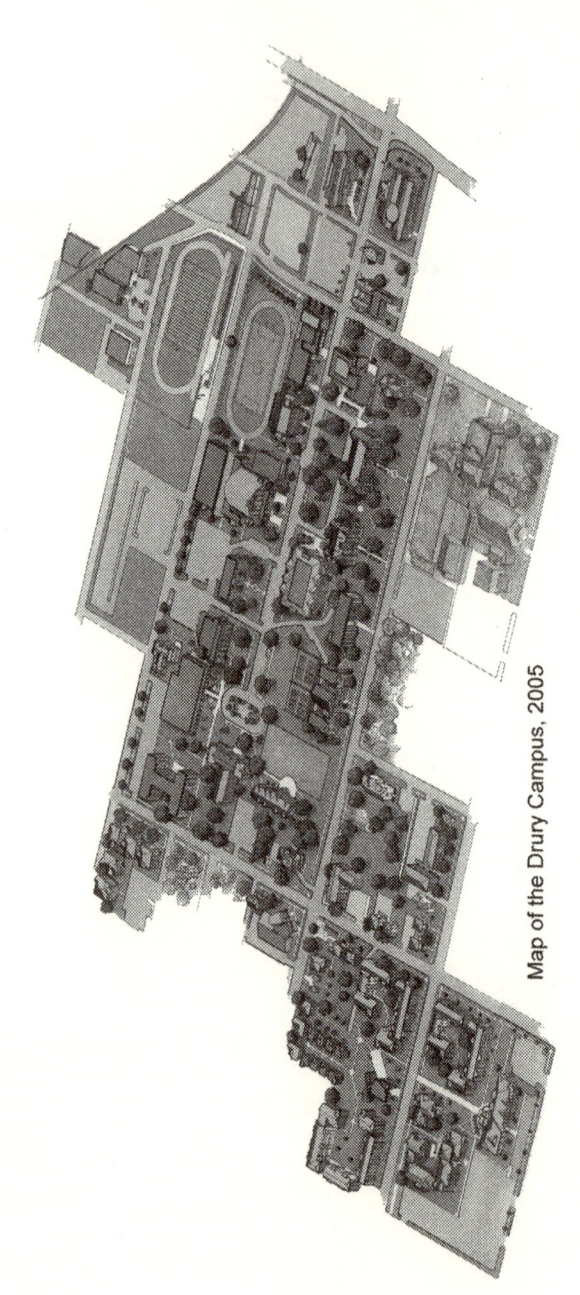

Map of the Drury Campus, 2005

In Memory of Steve Good

colleague, friend, mensch

# The Creation of a University:
# The Drury Story Continues
# 1977–2004

## Harvey Asher

From the Scholars Desk
Bolivar, Missouri
2007

Copyright ©2007 Drury University. All rights reserved. Printed in the United States of America. No part of this book may be used or reproduced in any manner whatsoever without written permission except in the case of brief quotations embodied in critical articles and reviews.

From The Scholars Desk
P.O. Box 34, Bolivar, MO 65613

www.fromthescholarsdesk.com/drury

Front cover photo by Paul Davis 2007
Back cover photo by Tristan Davies
Pictures on p. 146, 150 (right), 151 and 153 by Rebecca Miller

Paperback:
ISBN 1-931475-34-4
[ISBN 978-1-931475-33-4]

Hardback:
ISBN 1-931475-34-2
[ISBN 978-1-931475-34-1]

Second printing 4/2007

Library of Congress Control Number: 2007920955

# Contents

| | |
|---|---|
| Foreword | 9 |
| Introduction | 11 |
| Chapter 1 | 17 |
|    The Drury Story, 1873–1977: The East Comes West | |
| Chapter 2 | 39 |
|    The Tumultuous Years, 1977–1982: Shaking Up Drury | |
| Chapter 3 | 55 |
|    Men for All Seasons: John Moore and Steve Good | |
| Chapter 4 | 81 |
|    The Drury Difference | |
| Chapter 5 | 101 |
|    Student Life | |
| Chapter 6 | 121 |
|    Those Who Can Teach | |
| Chapter 7 | 135 |
|    It's More Than a Job | |
| Chapter 8 | 145 |
|    A Building Boom—Big is Beautiful | |
| Chapter 9 | 159 |
|    Into the Twenty-First Century | |
| Epilogue | 171 |
| Index | 175 |

# Foreword

Frank Clippinger's comprehensive history of Drury, *The Drury Story*, was published in 1982. It was the first book I read when I became Drury's fourteenth president in 1983. It is a good book, fascinating in parts, perhaps excessively detailed in others, but overall an essential reference on the course of this institution's history. It is a story filled with the hopes and commitment of men and women who have made up this place, the challenges, frustrations, and setbacks that have occurred all too regularly, and through it all the persistence and progress that have brought Drury University into its second century of service.

Some time ago, I perceived the need for a sequel to *The Drury Story* to deal with events of the last several decades. Much of this period has seen Drury's development—building on its traditional strengths in ways that have been remarkably gratifying. I felt this updated history needed as context the founding and broad sweep of Drury's earlier years. It also needed to be interpreted in terms of the people and events that have shaped Drury's more recent experience, again set in the larger context of American higher education in the late twentieth century.

Who to write this story, to interpret it in human terms and to bring skill and commitment to the task? My response was to recruit Harvey Asher, longtime professor of history at Drury, to the project. Dr. Asher joined the Drury faculty in 1967 and retired in 2003 after a successful career. A highly effective teacher and advisor to students, Harvey Asher has been one of the respected and much loved members of the Drury community. For years his inimitable sense of humor has lightened the faculty and staff and made us all chuckle. He continues to do so regularly via e-mail since retiring to Lancaster, Pennsylvania. But Harvey is also a serious scholar and competent historian, qualities I recognized in our visits about history, which was my own earlier academic area of interest. Harvey Asher was clearly the person for this job, and I'm grateful he agreed to take it on.

There were no rules or restrictions set down for Dr. Asher's charge other than what I've mentioned above as broad direction for the book. The result of his work in the pages that follow is a highly readable and fascinating story—often in personal terms—about the people who have made this institution what it is today. His book updates Clippinger's history and will be a standard reference about Drury, read and enjoyed by those who have studied here, who have labored here, and who hold this institution dear. I am pleased to commend Harvey Asher's book to you.

John E. Moore, Jr.<br>February 2005

# Introduction

When Drury University President John Moore first asked me sometime during the 2000–2001 academic year to consider bringing *The Drury Story* (1982) up-to-date—the book ended with the Board of Trustees' selection of Norman C. Crawford as Drury's thirteenth president on February 26, 1981—my answer was, "I'll think about it." Truth be told, I was being evasive, as the project initially held no great appeal for me. My impression, from the few college histories I had glanced at, was that either they veered toward institutional hagiography, sort of a scholarly public relations monograph, or they were encyclopedic in the amassing of factual detail; in either case, it seemed to me, they made for dull but informative reading for a narrow audience. More importantly, my own historical scholarship at the time, mostly about the Holocaust in the Soviet Union/Russia, was going well, relatively speaking, and I had no wish to be sidetracked.

Over the next six to nine months, when I encountered President Moore, usually for a Burnham hallway exchange of pleasantries, or conversations about a history book he had read recently—he is well acquainted with Clio, the muse of history, having majored in the subject as an undergraduate student—he would inquire as to whether I had given his proposal further thought. In retrospect, my new response, "I'm working on it," could be seen—it was—as being more receptive to his offer. I never felt pressured by him to say yes; his comments about the project stressed its importance and his excitement, and above all, his willingness to help. Subsequently I went to him in late 2002 and told him, "I'm ready to begin." I was not the first to succumb to a powerful John Moore left-right combination of charm and persistence.

My objective for the book is to continue telling the Drury story, which is not quite the same as recounting the history of the school.

My primary goal is to focus on those stories that best convey the essence of what the Drury experience is like for its most important constituency: its students, then and now. All those involved in making a Drury education possible, regardless of their positions in the school organizational chart, underscore that their ultimate goal is to serve the students. That is why the largest number of pages and two complete chapters in *The Creation of a University: The Drury Story Continues, 1977–2004* deal with all Drury students, including student-athletes, who in many college histories are given a separate chapter dealing exclusively with the institution's varsity sports.

From the members of the Drury community—faculty, administration, staff, alumni, friends—I tried to select those of their stories that illustrate what their contributions were to making this a better place for students to learn and develop into knowledgeable and caring citizens of the twenty-first century. I also chose stories that to me best encapsulate the Drury experience in a colorful or interesting way; consequently, many other worthy stories simply don't get told or at best receive fleeting mention.

While for the most part I proceeded chronologically, there are many instances where that is not the case. For example, I compressed Professor Oscar Fryer's story within a single section illuminating what he meant to Drury during his teaching years, and without pause continued the narrative from his retirement until his death at age 103. Similarly, parts of a chapter may be theme-driven, where dates play a peripheral role, such as in the discussion of curricular reforms. One beneficial result of shifting the focus between chronology and theme is that the individual chapters turned out to be "complete" stories in themselves and can be read nonsequentially.

I witnessed and participated in many of the events recounted in the book during my thirty-six years at Drury (1967–2003). That has both advantages and disadvantages. On the one hand, I can sometimes give an "insider's view," by going beyond the official account; more importantly, the passage of time allowed me the perspective to fit the particulars or daily happenings into a broader historical context. On the other hand, my lengthy career at Drury guarantees the accumulation of personal likes and dislikes, justifications and rationalizations that may color or bias my memory and vision. The best antidote for those liabilities is, as we historians like to say, to "go to the sources," critically analyze them, and compare the stories they tell with the ones contemporaries remember. I have tried to follow that advice as much as possible.

Chapter One provides a broad overview of Drury's place in the general development of private denominational higher education in the United States, followed by highlights of the Drury story from the founding of the college through the administration of President William Everheart that ended in 1976. Chapter Two tells of the troubled presidencies of John Bartholomy and Norman Crawford (1977–1982). Chapter Three discusses and analyzes the careers and ideas of Drury's two top leaders, President John Moore and Dean Stephen Good, during Drury's two remarkable decades under their leadership. Chapters Four and Five deal with the qualities of Drury College/University that make it a special place for students to learn and study, as well as describing what they do outside of the classroom, and how they evaluate their Drury experiences. Chapter Six recounts the contributions of the faculty and provides detailed biographies of two of its stalwarts. Chapter Seven explores the part staff—broadly defined—play in sustaining the Drury experience, and looks at those graduates whose connections to Drury span generations. The building boom on and off campus occupies most of Chapter Eight, while the final chapter deals with the challenges Drury faces in the twenty-first century, and its plans for meeting them.

## Acknowledgements

I would like to thank all of the following who agreed to extended interviews or provided valuable resources to me directly, and also those students in former communication professor Pat Brierton's Feature Writing class who conducted additional interviews and passed the information on to me: Joan Allen, John Beuerlein, Gale Boutwell, Loren Broaddus, Peter Browning, Virginia Bussey, Dan Cashel, Barb Cowherd, Krystal Compas, Robert Cox, Tristan Davies, Don Deeds, Darlene Dill, Brenda Elliot, Lisa Esposito, Eltjen Flikkema, Jay Garrott, Steve Good, Wally Grimm, Karolyn Holdren, John Holstrum, Paula McBurnett, Aaron Jones, Susan Kirby, Kevin Long, Vickie Luttrell, Sherrie Matthews, Maxim Matusevich, John Miller, Ruth Monroe, Jim Murrow, Stacey Naeger, Mike O'Brien, Chip Parker, Cliff Petty, Mary Jane Pool, Tim Posey, Lyle Reed, Red Richmond, Tiffany Roe, Rabindranath Roy, Melody Sanders, Rob Schraft, Pat Schreiner, Scotti Siebert, Tracy Sooter, Robin Sprenger, Karen Sweeney, Rob Weddle, Chuck Wells, Rusty Worley, and Roger Young. I remain acutely aware that because of considerations of space I have undoubtedly left out the names of many whose work ethos and pleasant dispositions make the Drury experience operate daily and long-term; you are greatly appreciated and respected.

Jim Buchholz and Bill Garvin both read drafts of the manuscript and called my attention to more than a handful of factual errors. Tristan Davies was instrumental in setting the book up for publication and for obtaining the wonderful photographs.

I am most grateful to John Moore and Pete Radecki for their crucial roles in getting the book published and to John Sellars and Drury University for their help in defraying its costs.

Thanks also to the following friends of the university for their generosity: E. Robert Breech, Jr.; Lloyd and Gale Boutwell; Jim and Marilyn Buchholz; Penny Clayton; Don Deeds; Betty Cole Dukert; Judy Good; Wally and Leigh Grimm; Don and Ruth Martin; Tom McAlear; Ruth Monroe; Jorge and Dorothy Padron; Tom and Jane Parker; Todd Parnell; Mary Jane Pool; Bill and Joyce Pyle; Bob Roach; Larry F. Robb; Rabin and Protima Roy; Jeff VanDenBerg; and Bill Wasson.

My wife, the author Sandy Asher, kindly interrupted her busy schedule to read various drafts and provide her usual thoughtful advice.

Special thanks to my editor, Ben Asher, whose suggestions immeasurably helped improve the organization, readability, and quality of the book. What deficiencies remain are mine. I hope they don't deter from my objective of having the book encourage continued pride in and support of Drury University by its readers.

*Sources*

In addition to Frank Clippinger (with Lisa Cooper), *The Drury Story* (1982), especially helpful for the first chapter were Roger Geiger, ed., *The American College in the 19th Century* (2000); C. J. Lucas, ed., *American Higher Education* (1994); George P. Schmidt, *The Liberal Arts College: A Chapter in American Social History* (1957); Donald Tewsbury, *The Founding of American Colleges and Universities Before the Civil War* (1932); and Charles Thwing, *A History of Higher Education in America* (1906). I looked at a number of recent college histories and particularly benefited from David Stameshkin's two-volume history of Middlebury College (1985, 1996).

The *Springfield News-Leader* and *Leader and Press* provided much valuable information, as did, of course, the *Drury Mirror, Drury Lane*, and its predecessor, the *Drury Quarterly*. I also benefited greatly from perusing the plethora of quality publications put out by the University Communications and Sports Information Offices, as well as the reams of departmental and Global Studies literature, reports of various assessment and self-study teams, and, for the story of Curt Strube, the *Springfield Business Journal*. John Moore and the late Provost Steve Good generously shared their personal papers. Dr. Moore gave me access to his ongoing correspondences with the Board of Trustees, which helped me to get a handle on his leadership style, while Dr. Good shared drafts of his papers that articulated subsequent ideas and policies that he advocated. I daily scoured the Drury Web site for up-to-date information. Statistical data came primarily from the offices of the registrar, the vice president for administration, and alumni and development. Jennifer Wiles's ('98) terrific senior Honors paper, "The

Drury Story: 1981–1983: The Crawford Years," proved invaluable; with her permission, I stole from it unabashedly. David Burton generously shared several articles he wrote on the ghost in Clara Thompson Hall while editor of the *Mirror* in the 1980s. The section on Professor Wayne Holmes owes much to Price Flanangan's extensive interview with him that appeared in the *Drury Quarterly* (Winter 1985). Jay Garrott's unpublished essay (2004) on the history of the Hammons School of Architecture, which he kindly shared, also was useful.

I have noted the sources where appropriate, but to maintain the narrative flow and stay consistent with *The Creation of a University's* goals both to inform and entertain, I chose not to use complete bibliographic citations in the text, and instead employed the less cumbersome Modern Language Association citation format; mostly, that meant not including the specific page numbers for newspaper and magazine stories. Quotations that appear without any citation most often came from the mind-boggling number of electronic sources about the university available through its Web site or from personal conversations. Occasionally, I have collapsed or altered the quote (mostly the verb tense) to keep the narrative flowing.

# Chapter 1

## The Drury Story, 1873–1977: The East Comes West

The Articles of Association of Drury College, first founded in 1873 as Springfield College, established as its mission "to afford to youth of both sexes ample facilities of instruction and discipline in those arts and sciences, a knowledge of which constitutes what is commonly known as 'liberal education,' by always maintaining in said college as comprehensive courses of study and as high standards of instruction and scholarship as prevail in other American colleges of the first rank, and at the same time to train youth in the high morality of the Christian religion."

While the new school replicated the experiences of most American frontier colleges—ties to a religious denomination, a curriculum integrating classical and modern courses, and constant struggling for fiscal solvency—Drury differed from many of its predecessors in two important ways: by being a coeducational institution from the start and by surviving.

Peter Browning, Drury chaplain and professor of religion and philosophy, believes that the founding of Drury by New England Congregationalists helped define the Christian identity on campus. Drury's New England fathers were abolitionists; hence there was a social justice commitment embedded in the institution from its inception. It was revealed in an early connection to the education of Native Americans, and in President Nathan Morrison's 1875 speech in which he argued that women had the right to a higher education. Mrs. Valerie Stone, a benefactor of Drury from Malden, Massachusetts, also gave significant money to Fisk, an all-black college.

In 1998, Drury College jubilantly celebrated its 125th anniversary, kicked off on September 23 by Drury archivist Bill Garvin's talk, "Dramatis Personae: A Look At the Key People Who Have Shaped Drury," at the annual Founders' Day program. This was the first in a yearlong series of events highlighted by the dedication of Quasquicentennial Plaza at the north end of Drury Lane. It had by no means been an easy journey for Drury to get to that joyful event, given the numerous obstacles it faced over the course of its existence: financial difficulties and small endowments, administrative instability, faculty conflict, and declining enrollments. How did Drury defy the odds that overwhelmingly predicted the school's likely demise?

## Pre–Civil War Antecedents

The vast majority of denominational colleges established before, during, and immediately after the Civil War sought to maintain the peculiarities of doctrine that distinguished them from their rivals. Their founders also hoped to advance learning and to perpetuate it for posterity. This seemingly broader goal included a strong religious dimension, inspired by the dread of having the church dominated by an illiterate ministry, for its clergy believed that learning and scholarship were essential for a proper understanding of God's handiwork.

It was this kind of vision and fear that inspired the Puritans (Congregationalists) to found Harvard, the first American college, in 1636. By the end of the colonial era (1636–1776), eight additional colleges existed in the English colonies; all but one had been founded under the sponsorship of churches. They included William & Mary and Columbia (Episcopalian), Dartmouth and Yale (by Congregationalists unhappy with Harvard's liberal theology), Princeton (Presbyterian), Rutgers (Dutch Reformed), and Brown (Baptist). Among these earliest institutions of higher learning, only the University of Pennsylvania had secular origins. Though the colleges' presidents usually came from the founding denomination, neither they nor their brethren monopolized the schools' governance, and the student bodies represented a variety of Christian denominations.

Although the growth of denominational colleges continued from the American Revolution until the end of the eighteenth century, the greatest spurt occurred in the nineteenth century. In addition to Eastern colleges such as Middlebury (1800) and Amherst (1825), new Western Congregationalist schools included Oberlin (1834), Knox

(1837), Grinnell (1847), and Ripon (1851). Many of the Western denominational colleges were beholden to the so-called second Great Awakening, a nationwide mass movement of evangelicalism and revivalism that began in the 1820s as a reaction to the establishment churches' neglect of their poorer members. Wending their way from the settled Eastern communities to the pioneer settlements on the frontier, the Great Awakening leaders saw the new colleges and churches as signs of the progress of Christian civilization, serving as agents of a mobile and growing population, while carrying the benefits of culture and religion to the remotest ends of the frontier. The new frontier colleges represented part of the revival of the forces of religion to combat what was perceived as the forces of evil infecting the rude frontier population. They were to do for the growing West what Harvard, Dartmouth, Amherst, etc., had done for New England: fashion a learned ministry and invigorate the entire system of popular education. Despite remaining grounded in their religious mission, the colleges maintained an all-inclusive public purpose, as would Drury.

The U.S. Census for 1860 listed 180 denominational colleges. The largest denominations were Methodist (34), Presbyterian (29), Baptist (25), and Congregationalist (21). The Congregationalist schools were less national in scope than the others, present in only twelve of the thirty-four states at the time of the Civil War. Approximately 81 percent of these colleges went belly-up shortly after their founding because of financial insolvency. Before closing their doors, many had offered little more than the rudiments of secondary education via a preparatory school attached to the college.

The question of where to locate the new colleges, as was also the case with Drury, became a matter of pride and competition among various communities. Often a lucrative offer of community support took precedence over geographic accessibility and even the concentration of coreligionists in choosing a school site. Fund-raising was crucial, as small numbers of students and low tuition made it impossible for the colleges to be self-supporting. Lack of revenue meant the Western Congregationalist colleges remained dependent on their Eastern connections for fund-raising. In turn, Eastern financiers encouraged the new Western schools to emulate the high academic standards of the older Eastern institutions. As most of the school sponsors were long on faith and short on cash, it often fell to the college president to find the funds to enable the institution to make it through another year, as most denominations hesitated to accept fiscal responsibility for their colleges, whose perennial deficits wreaked havoc on the churches' general budgets.

The earliest New England colleges followed the liberal arts curriculum, a program of study deemed essential for the education of ministers, gentlemen, statesmen, and the idle rich. Secular Greek and Latin writings dominated the curriculum because they represented the type of training the Puritan leaders had received at Cambridge and Oxford in England. These leaders remained convinced that the American ministerial elite should be exposed to nothing short of the best learning of the day. In contrast to the exclusive schools in England, the newer colleges subscribed to the notion that the average citizen was entitled to a chance at higher education best offered by regional and decentralized institutions of higher learning, whose graduates would be better Americans and democrats.

The widely circulated Yale Report of 1828 contended that the purpose of a liberal arts education was to allow individuals, by the free use of their faculties, to discover something about the meaning of the universe and man's (not yet woman's) place in it, and to promote the highest values men could obtain: mental discipline through the training of the intellect.

The Harvard curriculum, which served as a model for the other denominational colleges, devoted one-third of its courses to philosophy, which included physics, logic, and ethics. Also crucial was the study of Greek, as well as Hebrew for reading the Old Testament, considered the mark of an educated person. Mastery of Latin was not emphasized, for it was assumed entering students had already read the basic Latin texts in preparatory school; moreover, Latin was often the language for ordinary conversation at the university. The Harvard seal read, "*Christo et eccelesiae* [for Christ and His Church]," embodying the supremacy of character as the purpose of a liberal arts education, while embracing the old cardinal virtues of justice, temperance, and fortitude, as well as faith, hope, and charity.

Rhetoric, too, formed a significant part of the curriculum, as skill in public speaking was considered every bit as important as writing well. Mathematics usually occupied about one-fifteenth of the curriculum; interestingly, theology classes did not predominate the course of study. The objective of the curriculum, regardless of the graduate's intended vocation, was to produce thinkers, scholars, gentlemen, and worthy public servants. The use of the word *gentlemen* is not accidental, for the enrollment at the majority of colleges was exclusively male. By 1855, approximately ten thousand of the forty thousand graduates of American denominational colleges became ministers. The schools also turned out large numbers of physicians and lawyers.

In the infancy of the average college, there were usually not more than fifty men attending; the first coeds enrolled at Oberlin in 1833. Students were placed in classes according to distinction or the official rank their families held in the state. The same factors determined who got the most desirable campus living quarters. The average age of freshmen was usually between fifteen and sixteen, sometimes younger. College rules recommended that students pray in private, read scripture twice daily, and attend church regularly. Forbidden under threat of penalty was the use of profane or wanton words. Students could not leave town without parental permission. Regular attendance at faculty recitations was required. Other prohibitions included lying, improper dress, drunkenness, keeping guns, or firing pistols in the college yard. Violators were fined, the amount depending on the gravity of the offense. (For a listing of early regulations at Drury College, see "*In Loco Parentis*" below.)

The position of the freshman was particularly unenviable. Typically no freshman could speak to a senior while wearing a first-year cap. They were obliged to run errands for upperclassmen (except if deemed improper by the authorities). They also experienced what today we would call hazing. For example, a Harvard freshman who spoke unconvincingly at the introductory meeting held by seniors would be compelled to swallow a drink of salt and water. Or he might be required to swear an oath by kissing an old shoe. Worse, he might be tucked, which consisted of the senior making an incision with his fingernail on the freshman's lip.

In the nineteenth century, changes in college curricula included adding courses in history, economics, and romance languages, and placing more emphasis on mathematics and science. In part, the changes reflected growth in general human knowledge about these subjects, but also a lessening of the religious emotionalism of the Great Awakening, as well as greater national wealth and comfort. These curricular alterations were not always welcomed by academics and college presidents, who offered rigorous defenses of the traditional classical education, the only one they believed cultivated the branches of knowledge required for "those destined to a higher life." However, they lost the battle to keep the curriculum intact; by 1850 chemistry, botany, and even agricultural chemistry had entered the course of study.

The changes accelerated after the Civil War, as colleges came under increasing pressure to produce practical men to take charge of public roads, mines, railroads, and other institutions of a more industrial and urban America. The emphasis on mental discipline, the linchpin of the classical course, gave way to wider and more practical concerns. As entrepreneur Andrew Carnegie later explained, "College [classical] education as it exists is fatal to success in that domain." From the inclusion of new courses, it was a short hop to the elective system, where students chose most of their courses of study. As one prominent educator put it in the 1860s, "The young man of nineteen or twenty ought to know what he likes best and is most fit for." Furthermore, a Germanic influence brought back by graduates who studied abroad stressed the spirit of learning, teaching, and most significantly, the importance of scholarship. The curriculum at the German universities included philology, comparative literature, chemistry, economics, history, and psychology. Students could move from one university to another, attend class or not—ideas later embraced by American colleges.

During this period, instruction changed from one tutor teaching all subjects to a single class—segregated by rank—to a variety of tutors teaching subjects by academic discipline. Tutors listened to three recitations daily by their students, as the primary learning style was memorization. While under the old system ten faculty members sufficed to teach the classical course, the elective system required twenty-five teachers for the same number of students.

Phi Beta Kappa, the first college fraternity, came to William & Mary in 1776. Its initial purposes were patriotic and literary. Nearly fifty years later a spate of new national fraternities arose, becoming an integral part of college life; for example, Kappa Alpha in 1825 and Sigma Phi in 1827. Then as now, fraternities were both praised and condemned. Some admired the opportunities they offered for friendship among like-minded students, the encouragement of group responsibility, and school loyalty; others criticized their exclusivity, secrecy, and frivolity. Athletics also entered the student scene. At Harvard in 1827, football began its rise as the great American academic game. Yale housed the first rowing club (1843), and Princeton, the first baseball team (1858).

## *The College That Almost Wasn't—The Founders*

The story of where Drury fits into the history of denominational colleges—and higher education in general—is an interesting one, sometimes charged with high drama. As the vision of its four founders went from dream to reality, the process wasn't always smooth or easy, but rife with stories of high expectations and near catastrophe, of continuity and change, of bold challenges and seemingly insurmountable difficulties. But the Drury story is first and foremost the story of people, from presidents to deans, from faculty to students, and from staff to custodial workers, whose collective efforts, talents, and sacrifices not only enabled it to survive, but also, in time, to receive national recognition for its academic programs, while cultivating a sense of caring and community. That sense of inclusiveness remains on display today, whether an e-mail announcing the birth of a child, or a schoolwide signing of a get well or sympathy card. How did what is sometimes called the Drury Experience come to define the college?

In 1861, the year the Civil War began, Springfield, Missouri, with a population of around 2,500, was the largest and most prosperous town in southwest Missouri. By 1870, its population had more than doubled, spurred by the prosperity that accompanied the extension of the Frisco railroad line to the city in that year. A successful business district blossomed near the railroad tracks; it came to be known as

New Town or North Springfield. It was here that the soon-to-be-created new college would find its home.

The idea of establishing a Christian liberal arts college in southwest Missouri was the brainchild of the Springfield Association of Congregational Churches, many of whose members were graduates of Eastern Congregationalist liberal arts colleges. These New England denominational colleges would provide the model for Drury College. Drury's founders, atypically, were resolute that "There would be no ecclesiastical control, no orthodoxy," according to Jim Buchholz. ("Alumni Reunion," *Drury Lane*, Fall 1998.) Moreover, unlike colleges from other traditions, not until its thirty-sixth year did the academic study of religion occur at Drury, added only in 1909 when the Disciples of Christ assisted in establishing a Department of Religion and Philosophy. Drury has maintained a close relationship with the United Church of Christ, formerly the Congregational Church, since the school's inception, and with the Disciples of Christ since the establishment of the School of Religion. Both branches sustained traditions of a reasoned and critical approach to faith, as well as a heritage of progressive social action programs. The United Church and the Disciples of Christ, in their worldwide cooperative mission, focused primarily on service, communication, respect, mutual understanding, and appreciation, rather than conversion.

It was by no means certain that the new college would be located in Springfield. Two other strong contenders were the cities of Carthage and Neosho. Indeed, in a vote held in Pierce City in March 1873, Springfield barely edged out Neosho by one-half vote. The decisive vote was cast by Mrs. L. L. Allen of Pierce City. We don't know exactly why the Springfield location prevailed. We do know that it couldn't have done so without the efforts of two of the college's four founding fathers—the Reverend James H. Harwood (1837–1932) and his older brother, Judge Charles E. Harwood (1830–1933), both graduates of Williams College in Massachusetts. It was James Harwood, pastor of the First Congregational Church of Springfield, who organized the campaign to raise the necessary money for Springfield's bid; eventually he became the financial agent for the college. Subsequently he had little contact with the school, due to his disagreements (the details of which are unknown) with the first Drury College president. On the other hand, Charles, working from his Benton Avenue home, rallied the troops pushing to base the college in Springfield. He made a significant monetary pledge toward that end, and served as a trustee of the college for sixty years.

The third founder of the college, and its first president, was Nathan J. Morrison (1828–1907). An Easterner, he graduated from Dartmouth College, where he studied theology. He taught Greek and Latin at Oberlin College, and was ordained a pastor by the Congregationalist Church. In 1865, he became president of Olivet College in Michigan, but tensions with that school's trustees led to his resignation in 1872. At a meeting of a Congregational Church organization, he learned that a new college was about to be created in southwest Missouri. He soon visited Springfield, attended the Pierce City meeting where Springfield was chosen as the school site, and accepted the association's unanimous offer to be the new college's first president. He served until his resignation in 1887.

Samuel F. Drury (1816–1883) was the fourth founding father. Born in Spencer, Massachusetts, he left home at age fourteen and found work in Boston in a dry goods store. In 1838, he decided to seek his fortune in the West, and settled in Michigan, where he established a successful dry goods store. Through his membership in the Congregational Church, he became a fund-raiser for Olivet College, and later a member of its Board of Trustees. When Morrison resigned as Olivet's president, Samuel Drury encouraged him to look for an opportunity to organize another college, and offered him financial assistance toward that objective. Morrison, in turn, informed James Harwood that if Harwood could raise $50,000, Drury and his Eastern friends would match it. Morrison also indicated to Drury that he would take charge of the new college, and that in return for Drury's leading gift of $25,000, "the school will bear your [family] name" to honor Drury's son Albert, a member of the Olivet freshman class, who died in 1863.

However, at a March 1873 meeting, a misunderstanding among the new college's organizers threatened to bring the project to an abrupt close. Instead of cash, Samuel Drury decided to donate land; equally worrisome, he had not yet contacted his Eastern donors. Adding to the woes, the Springfield fund-raisers had only managed to obtain installment pledges, not the actual cash, from the would-be donors. The change from cash to land by Drury and the local shortfalls derived from the severe financial downturn that hit the country early in 1873. In any case, because there were no immediate funds on hand, it appeared all but certain the new college would not get off the ground. In fact, Samuel Drury was ready to withdraw completely from the project until friends convinced him otherwise.

Much to the chagrin of Drury, the Articles of Association adopted that March referred to the new school as Springfield College, the name used in the fund-raising campaign. However, as one newspaper reported, "It is determined to name the college Drury College, in honor of a gentleman who has taken a great interest in the enterprise." An amended charter of August 5, 1873, "founded" the college a second time as Drury. President Morrison, not wishing to alienate those who had pledged support to Springfield College, got Mr. Drury to defer the official name change until December 29, 1873, though advertisements using the name Drury College appeared in August.

Drury's origins, then, were hardly auspicious. It had barely obtained a Springfield location, its financial situation was tenuous, and conflict among the founders threatened the viability of the project. Differences aside, however, the founders shared a common vision cited in the Articles of Association, based on the charters of Olivet and similar schools, of creating a college for "the purpose of promoting the higher education and Christian culture." Unusual for the times, the articles designated Drury a coeducational institution.

Surprisingly, a provision of the articles limited trustees to four-year terms, suggesting President Morrison's caution about his past relationship with board members. No denominational restrictions were placed on students and faculty, though the Board of Trustees required a Congregationalist majority. That provision, as well as one prohibiting the college from acquiring any debt, did not last long. Whatever subsequent changes Drury experienced, the original mission remained at the heart of the school's purpose.

***

The organizers were now ready to find a campus site. Backers of the college came from the two rival parts of Springfield—Old Town (south and southwest) and New Town (north)—each wanting the college to grace its bailiwick. The dispute dissipated when the rival sides agreed the new college would be located "between towns." (By 1888, North Springfield was part of Midtown Springfield.)

The initial campus boundaries were Calhoun Street on the north, Benton Avenue on the west, Center Street (now Central) on the south, and Division Street (later Summit Avenue) on the east. It took sixteen years and an extra $20,000 to acquire the entire land parcel, as some existing homes had to be purchased before Drury became what has since affectionately been called "the Forty Acres." That nickname is still widely used today, though at this writing the campus spans more than eighty acres, and continues to expand.

Though the college was scheduled to open officially on September 15, a sense of urgency existed, as there was still no building available for the incoming class of thirty-nine students, which included eight women and seven Native Americans. The distinction of being the first person to seek admission to Drury College on September 10 or September 12 belongs to John Turner White, who graduated as the valedictorian in 1878. The first graduate of the college was Anna Grigg, who graduated in 1875. Efforts to procure a relatively new two-story public brick building built for the primarily black neighborhood students—in exchange for replacing it with a "better" structure—fell through because of objections from a mistrustful black community. Desperate, with no time for architectural planning, the school hired a contractor to copy the two-story building, and pushed back the school's opening to September 25.

\*\*\*

Like many of the early American colleges, Drury had a very small enrollment. The first class consisted of thirty-nine students and six faculty housed in a single building. The first faculty members included George Ashley and Paul Roulet—born in England and Switzerland, respectively, and educated in the East—who drafted courses of study covering both (college) preparatory and college requirements. The Bachelor of Arts program required two years of study in Greek, Latin, and mathematics. The third and fourth years included subjects from astronomy to English literature to zoology. A course in rhetoricals, which combined composition, rhetoric, and public speaking, also was required. The curriculum was consistent with the Drury vision of a liberal arts education as first articulated in the 1893 catalog: "To train the mind by a thorough, systematic classroom drill upon the leading departments of knowledge. The memory is first cultivated, and then the reasoning powers are developed, so that the student is taught to think for himself." The course of study, while rooted in the classical curriculum by its emphasis on the ancients and public speaking, also contained more "practical" subjects in response to the needs of industrialized and scientific America.

Nathan Morrison, the first president of Drury (1873–1887)

Over the next few years, President Morrison recruited new faculty primarily for their teaching skills. That some of them were not regular participants in Congregationalist affairs brought criticism from some of the local churches. Undaunted, Morrison worked on strengthening the academic environment, significantly upgrading the preparatory program, and building up library resources by soliciting donations from major publishing houses and Eastern Congregationalist ministers. His plans also called for a museum for instruction in the sciences to be headed by Professor Edward M. Shepard, who had obtained an extensive collection of animal, mineral, and plant specimens for it. At the end of the year, Morrison addressed the freshman class, telling them that the "college shall stand on a broader basis than party or sect—on the basis of Christianity, on the basis of humanity's Christ. She will take as the sentiment to engrave above her portals, the motto of the earliest-founded of American colleges—'*Christo et Ecclesiae*— for Christ and His Church'; nay, she will give this a broader, a nobler rendering—'*Christo et Humanitati*—for Christ and Humanity.'" This motto, expressed in print and in the second stanza of the school song, "Hail Alma Mater," is familiar to generations of Drury students, though not until 1909 did Professor Harrison Hales's lyrics gain widespread popularity.

*For Christ and Humanity,* according to Chaplain Browning, posits the relationship between faith and reason as not one of conflict but of mutual support. "To learn more about the sciences and humanities is to learn more about the nature and mystery of the created order. So there is no knowledge that is dangerous knowledge." *Christo et Humanitati* also suggests that God exists not only within the sacred texts, and within a community of faith, but also in the world. But more than respect and compassion for others was involved; the most important idea behind the motto was for Drury people to act and do, to sacrifice and serve the needs of others. Drury's latest mission statement of liberating persons to participate in and contribute to life in a global community fits in with its legacy of church affiliations by helping students clarify what it is they believe, and teaching them how to enter into respectful dialogue with people who have other points of view. It is interesting that President Morrison also saw the work of the school as one of reconciliation for "the horrid wounds of the Civil War."

\*\*\*

Morrison's original plan called for a college chapel. He eventually approached Valerie G. Stone, a friend of the college from Malden, Massachusetts, who had previously pledged $50,000 for endowment purposes. Miss Stone was a New England Congregationalist who funded institutions that offered educational opportunities for women, African-Americans, and Native Americans. She was persuaded to match an earlier gift procured by the Rev. James Harwood specifically earmarked for the college chapel; that her niece Ella Willcox was offered the job of principal of the Ladies' Department of Drury's Preparatory School (Willcox's predecessor resigned her position to marry Drury Professor Edward Shepard) likely contributed to her willingness to expand her generosity to the school by underwriting the construction of Stone Chapel, the oldest building on campus.

*Stone Chapel, the oldest extant building and spiritual center of Drury*

Miss Willcox's uncle suggested using stone from nearby quarries in Missouri rather than brick. President Morrison had faith that the additional costs would be borne, presumably, by Valerie Stone; unfortunately, she died soon after construction began. Then disaster struck on December 12, 1882, when Stone Chapel caught fire and was almost totally destroyed. The recently donated chapel crashed to the ground, though its bell was not damaged. The Board of Trustees, at its next meeting in 1883, voted unanimously to rebuild Stone Chapel as Morrison had planned. Morrison resigned as president of Drury in 1888 after the chapel was built; the furnishings of the auditorium and upper windows would be completed in 1891–1892. The class of 1892 was the first to hold its commencement in Stone Chapel.

In recent years Drury has held a fall Founders' Day convocation to honor its four founders and their successors, whose financial support helped Drury continue its mission. Invited to attend the event are current founders; that is, alumni and friends of Drury who have included the university in their wills, retirement plans, annuities, and trusts for at least $10,000.

## Ups and Downs

Throughout the 1880s, Morrison worked to acquire title to all of the campus property, while expanding enrollment, classroom space, and dormitories. The college managed to purchase the public school building it had sought ten years earlier. It became known as the East Academy Building, and its twin building became home to a science museum. These structures joined the first academic building, Fairbanks Hall, an elegant hall for women with some rooms for music and performing plays, underwritten by Charles Fairbanks, an American living in England whom a trustee won over as a friend to Drury. A frame house for male students known as Spencer Cottage went up near the museum in 1885, and after Morrison's resignation, his residence became home to unmarried faculty men.

The financial condition of the college worsened in the 1880s. Outside contributions tended to be small and there were difficulties converting land donations into cash. Grocery bills went unpaid and faculty salaries were paid in warrants. Construction projects came to a halt. In 1885, Morrison announced the college was $45,000 in debt. Under pressure by the board, Morrison resigned on June 15, 1887; his request to retain his professorship was denied. Clearly financial debt was an important factor in the board's loss of confidence in Morrison's leadership. Despite the gloomy turn of events, it is clear that Morrison was crucial in setting the tone and future direction of the college.

Morrison's successor, Francis T. Ingalls, had been pastor of the Congregational Church in Emporia, Kansas. He accepted the board's invitation to become president with the understanding that the trustees would take responsibility for finances. Ingalls turned the educational program over to the faculty, took on teaching responsibilities, and restored the friendship and support of Congregationalists in the area. Meanwhile, in 1891 the board launched an intensive fundraising campaign that succeeded in erasing all of the college's debt. Unfortunately, Ingalls became ill from exhaustion and died on August 15, 1892. Two professors served as interim presidents. Also, the Preparatory School became the Academy of Drury College, and partially separated from the college. In 1894–1895, the elective system entered the curriculum. These successes aside, Drury's financial situation remained precarious. It was a tuition-driven institution, and student fees simply did not cover educational costs.

*In Loco Parentis*

The first annual school catalog listed twenty general regulations for students; they included attending religious services, abstaining from alcohol and profanity, and avoiding billiards and bowling salons. Study hours and a 10:30 p.m. curfew were mandated. Violations of the rules resulted in demerits, called marks, which could lead to probation or expulsion. These kinds of restrictions on student life were hardly peculiar to Drury, for the purpose of the college was not just to dispense knowledge, but also to develop the character and responsibility of its students. At the turn of the century Emma Cooley came to Drury, where she worked as matron of Woodland Cottage, formerly President Morrison's home, and then a residence and dining hall. Drury Archivist Bill Garvin explains, "Mrs. Cooley was the guardian of [the female students'] moral well-being. She had to protect her girls from improper companions, idleness, vices of any sort, and, as the catalog phrased it, 'cheap fiction'" ("Dramatis Personae," *Drury Lane,* Spring 1999). Dancing was disallowed until the first campus dance, chaperoned by several trustees, took place on Thanksgiving of 1911. Women and men ate in separate dining rooms and sat on opposite sides in chapel. Class parties and picnics became popular in the 1890s. They were informal affairs with noisy games, including pranks between rival classes.

Drury students broadened the classroom experience by creating literary and musical societies, as well as political clubs. The first issue of the campus newspaper, the *Drury Mirror,* appeared in September 1886; the *Sou'wester* yearbook was unveiled in 1903. The *Mirror*'s first page had a literary emphasis, featuring a student story or prize oration. Editorials and campus news occupied the second page, humorous items ("personals") and the "Dormitory Hash" column made up the third, and advertisements the last. Drury's first honor society, the Skiff-Mortar Board, was founded in 1914 to reward junior class women for scholarship, leadership, and service.

Baseball was first initiated in the late 1880s. However, the campus athletic program started with the organization of the football team in 1890; it wore the school's colors—scarlet and gray—in its first season. Track came in 1902, followed by basketball and tennis. In the fall of 1906, Drury adopted the panther as its mascot because, as reported in the *Mirror,* "If the first blow fails he is not discouraged but fights harder and fiercer than before."

As You Like It, *1901*

Dramatics became a cocurricular activity in 1887 and debate teams formed, a shift from the emphasis on formal oration that played such a prominent role in the earliest curriculum. Nonetheless, each graduating senior continued to deliver an oration as part of the commencement exercises.

Kappa Alpha was the first national fraternity on the Drury campus (1907), followed in short order by two sororities, Pi Beta Phi and Zeta Tau Alpha. By 1911, there were six Greek organizations on campus, three for men and three for women. Their membership constituted roughly half the student body, a relatively steady figure until the 1980s.

\*\*\*

Between 1894 and 1917, Drury had five different presidents, none of whom was terribly successful; at one point the Board of Trustees ran the college. The revolving presidency ended with the appointment of Thomas W. Nadal to the office on March 29, 1917. He inherited a gloomy economic situation where operating costs continued to exceed income, although the school had obtained some funding from the Carnegie Foundation. These funds had been contingent on two conditions: Drury had to rescind the requirement that a majority of trustees be Congregationalists and had to separate the Drury Academy from the College. By 1912, it had met both conditions.

There were several successful construction projects during this time period, including Pearsons Hall (1901); a gymnasium (1909); Burnham Hall (1910), home to the administrative offices and the

Classics Department; and a dining commons and boiler plant. Also, the curriculum changed. The 1907–1908 catalog listed the classical path as only one of several options. Other choices offered were science, pre-med, history, and philosophy. Shortly thereafter music, pre-engineering, education, and teacher certification programs joined the list. While Drury's mission and goals remained centered on studying the liberal arts in a Christian environment, the academic paths to that end had widened considerably.

## In Search of a President

Thomas Nadal, Drury's seventh president, came from Olivet College, where he began as professor of English and advanced to acting president. He was elected shortly before the United States declared war on Germany in April 1917. On the Drury campus, where students preferred to volunteer rather than await the draft, only eight men remained in the 1917–1918 senior class; overall enrollment dropped by ten percent. Nadal came to Drury determined to raise half a million dollars for the general endowment. He put in place a comprehensive plan by June 1919 and secured adequate pledges within a year. Strikingly, Nadal was not inaugurated as president until three years after his appointment, preferring postponement until "he had accomplished something worthwhile." Commencement in 1924, Drury's fifty-first anniversary, brought Nadal's announcement that the endowment exceeded a million dollars, debts had been erased, and the much-awaited library would be built.

In 1926 alone, three new buildings adorned the campus: the Wallace Hall dormitory, the Harwood Library, and the Clara Thompson Hall of Music. Between 1920 and 1924, the student body went from 272 to 411, leading the board to recommend more selective admissions. Enrollment numbers continued to rise, reaching 480 in 1929. At the same time, the rapidly expanding curriculum increasingly emphasized contemporary subjects and no longer required Greek and Latin.

Student life was vibrant. During the 1920s, the Student Senate became firmly established as the coordinator of student activities, the *Mirror* discontinued its literary emphasis in favor of a hard news format, the Seven Sages society recognized its members' academic performance, and other new honor societies heralded student achievement in various academic disciplines. The first Homecoming was held in 1924.

Drury's version of the Roaring Twenties arrived gradually. Cigarette smoking became popular and party games gave way to dancing, at least for upperclassmen. Dancing guidelines specified complete avoidance of bodily contact, and required couples to remain in view of the chaperones. Jazz was banned at all college functions. Women still needed permission to dine in public with men or to attend Sunday movies. Chaperones were required for women using an automobile or visiting men's residences. The end of formal dress codes for dining at the Commons took place in the 1960s, following the retirement of Drury's eighth president, James L. Findlay. Chapel remained mandatory, though men and women could now sit there together.

Athletic programs flourished under the direction of coach Albert L. Weiser, who came to Drury in 1927 and remained as athletic director until 1963. Tennis and golf were added to the intercollegiate athletic program. Weiser's basketball teams claimed three league championships in a row from 1936 to 1938. Today's fans continue to flock to Weiser Gymnasium, home to both the men's and women's basketball teams.

## Financial Woes Return

Drury's expansion in the 1920s came to a halt when the Great Depression swept across the country. The board was shocked to learn from a Price-Waterhouse audit that no system existed at the school to keep endowment funds separate from general ones: The endowment was $400,000 in arrears. That debacle, together with a Depression-induced enrollment decline, called for drastic economies. The school laid off many campus workers and shut off heat and light in unused areas. Faculty loads increased and their salaries were reduced, as was President Nadal's. The football program was eliminated; it never returned.

Predictably, the Nadal "honeymoon" was over. Rumors circulated of high student turnover and unqualified new faculty. Alumni complained of unrealistic recruitment standards for athletes and mailed an angry circular to the Alumni Association, describing Drury as "sliding backward down hill," and demanding Nadal's resignation. Nadal survived the initial onslaught, but a second assault by another alumni group in 1939 led to a board resolution calling for his retirement the next year.

## Golden Years

On April 12, 1940, Dr. James F. Findlay succeeded the forced-out President Nadal. A former Congregationalist minister, he had served as dean of men at the University of Oklahoma. His plans for Drury called for increasing enrollment, improving student and faculty morale, and eliminating the budget deficit. His inaugural address, entitled "The 'Whole' College Educates the 'Whole' Student," established the Drury Plan of personalized education, emphasizing individual goals, conscientious academic advising, and a lessening in the number of required courses. Within a year all the Findlay objectives were met.

*James Findlay, the eighth president of Drury (1940–1964)*

On December 7, 1941, came Pearl Harbor. The campus participated in many war-related activities: the Red Cross, the Burge School of Nursing, and training in medical and X-ray technology. McCullagh Cottage and Fairbanks Hall became barracks for enlisted men who were sent to Drury for a ten-week aviation course before being summoned to active duty. In recognition of Drury's war efforts, the United States Maritime Commission christened a war-tested cargo ship SS *Drury Victory*.

Unique among Missouri colleges, Drury's enrollments actually increased during and immediately after World War II, aided by an aggressive recruiting program and early admission of high school students and veterans without diplomas. The upswing continued after the war; between 1945 and 1950 enrollment soared from 479 to 901, even with an upgrade in admission requirements. Campus construction projects abounded. An airplane hangar was converted into the new gymnasium; a new dorm, Belle Hall, was built to house women; the chapel interior was completely renovated. Trustee Lester E. Cox made possible an illuminated fountain at the end of Drury Lane. Also contributing to the upsurge was the evening college, the first in southwest Missouri, implemented in 1947 under the guidance of Business Professor Wilber E. Bothwell—"Buzzy" to his friends.

Other Findlay building projects included Turner Hall (1948), an addition to Wallace Hall (1956), Walker Library (1959), the Breech Building (1961), Sunderland Hall (1961), and Atha Pool (1961).

Drury's Diamond Jubilee in 1948 occasioned a series of special events, culminating in four days of festivities at Commencement. Dr. Lewis E. Meador, professor of government, chaired the seventy-fifth anniversary committee, as he had the fiftieth. The following year, composers Richard Rodgers and Oscar Hammerstein II received honorary degrees on campus, an event covered on national television by ABC.

## Musical Presidents

After directing the progress of the college for nearly a quarter of a century, President Findlay retired in 1964. A 1943 *Mirror* story had said of him, "Community respected, yet not formidable, the President of Drury College has won a place in the hearts of Drury students as their counselor and friend." After leaving Drury, he went to the School of the Ozarks, where he served as a dean until 1969. When he died in 1987, Drury held a special service in Stone Chapel in recognition of his contributions to the college.

Dr. Earnest Brandenburg, a dean at Washington University, was named his successor. Brandenburg believed Drury needed to expand its reach to the surrounding states, implement a more selective admissions policy, hire more faculty, give long-delayed pay raises to current faculty, and expand the faculty's role in policy formulation. These goals were either accomplished, or on their way to being so, when in March 1967 Brandenburg died of cancer. In his short tenure, he had earned the respect and admiration of all Drury constituencies, especially the faculty, who considered him their advocate.

Former dean Frank W. Clippinger was coaxed from retirement to serve as acting president after Brandenburg's death. Enrollment reached a record high of 1,200 students that year, and for the first time the annual school budget exceeded $2 million. In November 1967, the board named Alfred O. Canon from Southwestern College in Memphis (Rhodes College) as the new president. Faculty morale soared as Canon pushed for increased fringe benefits, to be paid for by tuition increases, and a new tenure policy. The Lay Science Center was dedicated in the spring of 1969 and McCullagh Cottage was razed in anticipation of a new student center dining hall. Unfortunately, student attrition at Drury soon increased appreciably, part of a wider national trend influenced by the Vietnam War. Because the college ran a deficit in 1969, President Canon was forced to cut fourteen faculty; those spared received no pay raises for the next few years. By 1970, Canon was gone, dismissed by the board at an April meeting. Long-term administrator and business manager Carl Stillwell was in charge of the college until a permanent replacement for Canon was found. He inherited a campus of disgruntled faculty and regular deficits.

In February 1971, Dr. William E. Everheart, a Drury trustee who had served as senior minister of a Presbyterian church, became the college's new president. That he had been a member of the presidential search committee to select Canon's replacement caused controversy. The financial situation remained fragile: More faculty layoffs occurred and money was borrowed to cover operating expenses. Despite the school's struggle with mounting financial deficits and declining enrollments, Drury began its yearlong centennial celebration on September 25, 1973, with the dedication of the Findlay Student Center. The college also paid tribute to the many accomplishments of Dr. Lewis E. Meador, named "Springfieldian of the Twentieth Century" by the Chamber of Commerce. On a windswept day, comedian Bob Hope delivered Drury's one-hundredth commencement address.

The high inflation of the 1970s and a shortage of college-age students worsened matters for Drury and other private colleges, many of which went out of business. Drury's misfortunes continued when, in 1976, President Everheart died in a car-train crash. Dr. Jorge L. Padron, academic dean and professor of chemistry, served as acting president until Dr. John Bartholomy, a Murray State University administrator, took over in January 1977. Would the new president stay long enough to provide the administrative stability the college so sorely needed?

### Student Grumblings

Drury students reacted to some of the political and social upheaval of the late 1960s and early 1970s, albeit in a limited manner. At the Founders' Day held during Drury's 125th anniversary, 1960s graduate Lynn Chipperfield remembered that the social environment of the late 1960s and early 1970s was quite interesting. As he put it, "If you remember the '60s, you weren't really there" (*Drury Lane*, Spring 1999). Small nonviolent anti–Vietnam War marches and debates in Stone Chapel occurred in 1968–1969. There was a candlelight vigil to protest the 1970 shooting of students at Kent State University by National Guardsmen. *Mirror* editorials, mostly written by future student body president Rick Ayre, and later Randy McConnell, expressed opposition to the Vietnam War and support for the civil rights movement. The paper published a letter from a Vietnam vet, a Drury alumnus, that used a curse word. Outrage from President Canon and the Board of Trustees led the Publications Committee to ban permanently the use of four-letter words in school publications. In response, the *Mirror* caricatured the school president, who then announced that alumni, parents, and prospective students would no longer receive copies of the *Mirror*, but instead would be sent copies of a new publication, the *Drury Quarterly*.

The *Mirror* also lobbied successfully against compulsory chapel, and supported the Student Senate's efforts to overturn dress codes and loosen curfews. In 1968, students of legal age (twenty-one) received permission to consume alcohol in the dorms. Further controversy ensued in 1971 when the Student Union Board invited political activist William Kunstler to campus. Board displeasure with the choice led to several postponements of his lecture, until Kunstler offered his own property bond and agreed to waive his fee.

The politically neutral and disengaged constituted a majority at Drury, as they did nationwide. Nonpolitical students might listen to or play in Professor Don Verne Joseph's Drury Jazz Swingers, attend musician Stan Kenton's summer jazz festival, or participate in the Drury Singers, who launched their first European concert tour under the direction of Professor Darrell Benne. Or they could experience the new housing policies, championed by Sue West ('75), the first woman student body president, by choosing to live off campus or use their own discretion to return to the dorms after-hours unless their parents objected to the venture in writing. Also available were the traditional standbys: studying and goofing off.

In the late 1970s and early 1980s, a different kind of politics, involving Drury administrators and faculty, would greatly affect morale on campus.

# Chapter 2

## The Tumultuous Years, 1977–1982: Shaking Up Drury

John M. Bartholomy, named Drury's twelfth president in January 1977, assumed his duties on March 1. Previously Dr. Bartholomy had served as vice president of university services at Murray State University in Kentucky. He held a Ph.D. in speech pathology from Ohio State University. He received the unanimous support of the presidential search committee, which praised his abilities as an administrator and fund-raiser. He would need those skills, for the college's debt stood between $600,000 to $800,000. Shortly after he arrived, he pledged to the Drury community that he would always be candid with them.

In April, Lee Rowell resigned as admissions director; enrollments in 1976 had declined by 45 students from the previous year's figure of 869; the slide in student numbers also reflected a 19 percent attrition rate. President Bartholomy set up a Presidential Task Force on Admissions and Attrition to address the problem. To help improve its financial situation, Drury agreed to house 73 Southwest Missouri State University undergraduates in Fairbanks Hall when SMSU had run out of on-campus housing for its entering class. Bartholomy eliminated a number of administrative and staff positions: the vice president for development and the associate dean and their secretaries; two workers, one in the Registrar's Office, the other in the library; and another whose name "I do not want to release now, because I have not notified that person yet."

In an interview with the *Mirror*, President Bartholomy told the reporter he would not become involved in the faculty cuts that had been proposed before his arrival, though his statement that "We have less than eight hundred students and we've been staffed at a level for a thousand" was not reassuring (March 3, 1977). Also worrisome to the faculty were these words by the new president: "Let me be candid and honest with you—we've cut our faculty, we've tried to cut more than we could successfully pull off in a short period of time. I have to wait a year before I can cut faculty that will keep me out of court, in a respectable way, in a gentlemanly way."

*John Bartholomy, the twelfth president of Drury (1977–1980)*

A day earlier, he had introduced at a faculty meeting what he called the Bartholomy Test of Teaching Excellence (BTTE). It contained nine questions:

1. Is the learning environment you create worth four times the tuition paid by SMSU students?
2. Is your teaching judged first-class by your students, department chair, and dean of the college?
3. Are all your lecture notes less than three years old?
4. Have you been on a student recruitment trip in the last three semesters?
5. Did you have ten students in your office last week receiving personalized education?

6. Are you reading at least three books and the major journal in your field each semester?
7. Do you possess the terminal degree in your field?
8. Were you invited to speak to three community groups last semester or have you submitted two manuscripts to respected journals in your area?
9. Do you promote student use of the library?

He went on to pledge his willingness to fight for faculty raises but insisted, "If you have not passed the Bartholomy Test, I will not reward poor or mediocre teaching at Drury. All the big raises will go to talented teachers that are producing. I am not going to reward average teachers." Bartholomy later told a *Sou'wester* reporter "that he had evaluated the faculty before he moved onto campus, dividing them into doers and nondoers" (1980, 158).

The decline in student numbers also led to budget cuts for the Student Union Board, the *Mirror*, the *Sou'wester*, and KULR, the student radio station. Bartholomy also appointed a task force to review the scope and role of the evening college, wanting to create a Drury College "that opens its doors to all students—8 [a.m.] to 10 [p.m.] daily." A November 17, 1978, *Mirror* editorial questioned the wisdom of the move, cautioning that the Continuing Education Division had good enrollments that might be adversely impacted by the proposed dramatic change. His proposal also stirred up the perennially contentious question of what the relationship between day and evening programs should be.

The cost-cutting measures went hand in hand with six weeks of preparation for Bartholomy's inauguration, scheduled for October 8. Preludes to the inauguration included concerts, a presentation of *Dark of the Moon* by the newly created Department of Fine Arts (combining the music and theatre departments), and the President's Ball, preceded by Drury Choir and Drury-Evangel Orchestra performances. At the inaugural, some speakers warned of problems facing private colleges, but they also spoke of the satisfaction that President Bartholomy might gain by helping guide Drury during those rough times (*Springfield Leader and Press*, October 9, 1977). Drury Alumni President Charles Tillman ventured that he was impressed with the actions already taken by Bartholomy. "If the first few months are any indication, the next few years will be bright." Dean of the Faculty Jorge Padron spoke of new hope among the faculty. "All of us have been inspired to be better teachers by Bartholomy's expectations for faculty." "I believe in him and in Drury," added Student Senate President Phil Page. Despite all the hard work and hoopla preparing for the inaugural, the postinauguration *Mirror* editorial lamented the sparse student attendance at the events preceded it.

The Bartholomy years witnessed a major revision of the curriculum under the direction of Dean of Faculty Allen Eikner, a change as extensive as the one in 1941 that first introduced the Drury Plan of personalized education. Adopted in 1978, the new curriculum called for enlarging subject area distribution requirements for graduation. It mandated that students take classes in each of four areas of knowledge. *Cultural Heritage* included courses in Western civilization, foreign languages, non-Western culture, and written composition. *Modes of Inquiry* focused on the different methodologies employed in math, science, and the social sciences. *Contemporary Issues* dealt with current issues and developments. *Personal Development* classes emphasized the stimulation of student creativity through exposure to music, theatre, and the fine arts. A month-long Winter Term, held between semesters, encouraged student participation in specially created "unusual" courses, independent research, and travel abroad.

The idea behind the reform was to assure that Drury students achieved proficiency in writing, speaking, mathematics and logic, and foreign languages. It also was a reaction to the loosely structured curricula that had been in vogue nationally and at Drury during the turbulent 1960s, when students reacted to the Vietnam War and the civil rights movements by demanding their schools offer classes—the buzzword was *relevant*—that addressed their concerns, rather than following a curriculum where one size fit all.

Students of the 1960s were highly critical of their elders; academically that translated into a shunning of the ancients—the Dead White Males—whose classical writings formed the core of the traditional curriculum that was now deemed antiquated and irrelevant. The prevailing student norms prioritized the centricity of individual need over societal concerns, and the right to choose courses and programs that gratified the sovereignty of the individual. As student activism faded in the late 1960s, Drury returned to a more structured curriculum.

*False Hopes*

In November 1977, following a feeling-out visit by Dean Jorge Padron and Professor of Business Charles Mercer, Dr. B, as many called Bartholomy, flew to Teheran, Iran on a "fact-finding mission" to see about the possibility of establishing a Drury branch there. The Mahvi Educational Foundation, several of whose family members graduated from Drury, proposed to donate $100,000 to Drury through a deposit in an endowment fund. Thirty Iranian students would study at Drury and pay full tuition. The faculty unanimously approved of the plan. Bartholomy announced, "Drury will have the first Western-oriented liberal arts college in Iran by the fall of 1978." The *Mirror* opined that the additional monies "could be substantial enough to be 'the saving grace' for the Drury financial picture." Shortly thereafter, Ayatollah Khomeini seized power in Iran, stirring up vehement anti-Americanism that led to the hostage crisis in 1979. That event led to Bartholomy's subsequent announcement: "I am not optimistic we will see a Drury College in Iran."

## A Polarized Campus

In January 1978, Bartholomy appointed an administrative council that included ten department chairs. Those chairs not chosen to serve complained that he showed favoritism in this and in other decisions, creating divisiveness among the faculty and departments. When a popular economics professor was dismissed from his position at mid-semester, faculty disgruntlement grew, although the faculty review board affirmed the decision. After the college received a $500,000 construction gift from the Lydy Foundation, Bartholomy's comment that Drury did not need a new building irritated some. He proposed as an alternative that the money be used to establish Lydy Presidential Scholarships, to be paid for from the interest on Drury's endowment, the grants to include full tuition, room and board, and books. In April 1978, Bartholomy announced the first winners of the Lydy Presidential Scholarships: Thomas Barton, Mark Cascairo, Jodie Kahut, and David Peeples.

The new scholarships fit in with Bartholomy's earlier plan to offer, with the help of the Board of Trustees, seventy-five academic scholarships valued at $2,175 (the tuition at the time) to talented students, who otherwise would not attend Drury, and whose American College Test (ACT) scores were above average. The scholarships would be distributed to departments whose faculty actively engaged in recruiting new students, "because I will be defeating my purpose if they go to the 280 students already planning on coming. If I can raise 200 of those this year and 200 next year, we are out of debt, comfortably." The plan also called for each of the classes—freshman, sophomore, etc.—to raise a $2,175 scholarship, and challenged the faculty to match them. Conjectured Bartholomy, "I think the sophomores are going to win because I think they are more resourceful than juniors or seniors, and I hope you put that in your article." The president also unveiled a proposal for Drury to match dollar-for-dollar monies new students acquired from other private scholarships. He also promised them he would fight raising tuition.

By the fall of 1979, the president and his wife, Mary Jo, had moved from the house on North Benton Avenue, serving since 1895 as the president's residence, to a new home in the Oak Knolls area of Springfield. In a September *Mirror* interview, President Bartholomy reported that their on-campus residence had been the site of two robberies and one act of vandalism, resulting in the loss of $11,000 in stolen property. Their newspaper vanished at least once weekly; loud fraternity parties and blasting stereos permeated their private space. An anonymous $50,000 gift paid for the Bartholomy's new domicile. It was contingent on the demolition of the presidential home, built in 1895 for $7,000, and its replacement by a parking lot. Bartholomy, the first-ever Drury president to reside off-campus, reported a few months later, "We are now more relaxed and not worried to be alone in our new home." The move and the plans for demolishing the Benton Avenue residence engendered controversy. The *Mirror* ran a series of letters from students on this issue; most asserted, "We should not tear up a part of Drury's tradition;" some disagreed: "We could use a parking lot." A popular T-shirt worn on campus read on its front side, THE PRESIDENT SHOULD BE RESIDENT, and on the back, SAVE 1234 NORTH BENTON.

The president's policies frightened many faculty, who found them adversarial and demeaning, and most importantly, threatening to their job security. Perhaps most decisive, in the judgment of his critics, was the manner in which his policies were presented. They considered the process beset by favoritism, and saw it as contributing to faculty polarization. His supporters thought that his shakeup was the only way to combat faculty lethargy, smugness, and cliques that prevented the upgrading of a Drury education needed for a competitive student recruitment market. For them, his emphasis on merit pay was long overdue.

Particularly explosive was the new list of expectations for department chairmen—replaced in the 1980s by the gender-neutral terms *department head* and *department chair*. Among its most controversial items was the requirement that chairs observe all departmental professors in the classroom at least twice each semester and submit written reports to the dean and the professor. It mandated that the department head handle the following kinds of disciplinary measures: verbal reprimands, written warnings, withholding favorable recommendations for committee assignments, withholding travel money or other benefits, and removal of a faculty member from the classroom or other contacts with students.

At a special meeting held on April 19, 1978, a group of faculty discussed the prospect of enlisting the American Association of University Professors (AAUP) as its collective bargaining agent. Students present were asked to leave before a vote was taken. Physics Professor James Riley was the president of the Drury chapter of the AAUP, whose members made up a majority of a group of faculty that proceeded to solicit the support of the entire faculty to unionize, that is, to acquire the right to bargain collectively with the Drury administration. Over the next several months the campus became a hotbed of political intrigue as pro- and antiunion factions tried to line up votes for the scheduled election to be held under the jurisdiction of the federal government's National Labor Relations Board (NLRB). Almost daily, if not hourly, the rival groups held meetings to solidify and expand their supporters, and to stack important faculty committees with their patrons. The tension and bitterness on campus was palpable; long-term friendships among faculty teetered on the brink of dissolution; some succumbed.

The NLRB hearings determined there were sixty eligible faculty voters. A simple majority vote meant the AAUP would be certified as the faculty representative, eligible immediately to initiate negotiations with the administration. Both sides raised voter eligibility challenges, eleven in all: Had the faculty person signed a contract by the election date? What division of the college did the employee work for, day or evening? The disputed ballots were set aside prior to the counting of the vote held on June 22, 1978. The election results: twenty-six for the union, twenty-three against. The closeness reflected the acute polarization—just about down the middle—of the faculty. On August 7, 1978, the NLRB hearing officer recommended that objections to the exclusion of four professors' ballots be overruled—two of them supported the AAUP and two were for the administration. Seven other ballot exclusions were sustained. Both sides could file objections to the decision but did not do so. Drury had become a union-recognized college. But would the administration negotiate with the union as the faculty's collective bargaining agent? And what if it refused to do so? Would that mean censure by the AAUP?

*Calm Before the Storm*

The Bartholomy years also witnessed some positive developments for the school. In welcoming students back for the 1978–1979 academic year, President Bartholomy announced the recruitment of the second-largest freshman class in Drury's history. (In 1977, President John Bartholomy had named Dr. Eltjen Flikkema director of admissions. Under Flikkema between 1977 and 1980, enrollments jumped from 981 to 1,132.) First-time freshmen and freshman transfers combined numbered 393 new students, contributing to a total head count of 983. "During the past eighteen months, I've frequently told you that Drury College needed nine hundred students to be cost-effective; it sure seems good to have reached that level." The 1979 Cinderella year when the men's basketball team won the National Association of Intercollegiate Athletics (NAIA) championship, the first-ever Drury athletic team to win a national title, provided great joy to the Drury community, and fostered feelings of togetherness. October 16, 1979, saw the dedication of the Lydy-O'Bannon Center, consisting of a remodeled Clara Thompson Hall, with two adjacent wings on its sides—the O'Bannon Music Center to the north and the Lydy Art Center to the south. The refurbishing of the concert hall in Clara Thompson was made possible by a gift from Dorothy O'Bannon, sister of Drury alumnus George O'Bannon. Bartholomy also procured a $484,000 grant from the J. L. Mabee Foundation, which the college had to and did match, allowing for the construction of the two additions.

Bartholomy appointed Professor Riley to chair a Task Force on Energy to find ways to reduce the exponential rise in energy costs at Drury, created in part by the Mideast oil embargo. The Riley group recommendations resulted in measurable savings for the college. Likewise Bartholomy's appointment of Judy Martin as vice president of alumni and development resulted in a sharp rise in gifts and giving for the college.

## *Out of the Frying Pan*

John Bartholomy abruptly resigned his presidency at Drury in May 1980 to accept a similar position at William Woods College in Fulton, Missouri. For a second time, Dr. Jorge Padron agreed to serve as Drury's acting president. During his earlier brief tenure, Dr. Padron had secured the renovation of the Campus Exchange (CX), the opening of Weiser Gymnasium to students, and a commitment to renovate the band building. He pledged "not to allow any department to slide." The opinions column of the *Mirror* endorsed Padron's candidacy to become Bartholomy's permanent successor, editorializing that "Dr. Padron was the most logical choice to replace Bartholomy because he was a man who understood that what made Drury different was its liberal arts atmosphere" (February 20, 1981). It cited an article in the *Springfield Leader and Press* that Drury "students and faculty didn't seem too concerned about the void created by Dr. Bartholomy because Dr. Padron had more than filled that void."

*Jorge Padron, Dean of the College and twice acting president*

*Norman Crawford, the thirteenth president of Drury (1981–1983)*

The *Mirror*'s advice did not prevail. Judy Martin, a member of the presidential search committee to choose Bartholomy's replacement, later said the primary reason for not choosing Padron was health concerns about him—he suffered from heart problems—but she also indicated that hiring an internal candidate was extremely difficult. This writer, who served on the search committee, remembers that some members raised doubts as to whether Padron, who spoke with a heavy Spanish accent, projected the right image for Drury in the community and before grant-bestowing institutions. It should be stressed that it was the public speaking skills and not the ethnicity of Padron that was at issue.

Dr. Norman C. Crawford, Jr., became the choice of the Board of Trustees, and he flew to Springfield for an interview. Following that visit, the search committee, consisting of three board members, two faculty, one administrator, and one student, asked Crawford's permission to visit Salisbury State in Maryland, where he had served as president the past ten years before being asked to resign by its Board of Regents, allegedly because the school had a $500,000 budget deficit. Crawford believed the decision by the regents was unfair; the president of another college the board oversaw was not dismissed despite running a deficit at his school of more than $1 million. Specifically, Crawford attributed his termination to his fight for a larger share of state funding for Salisbury State, as the school had little political clout when it came to state monies.

During the visit, the committee attempted to check out rumors about Crawford's tenure at Salisbury State. One that circulated claimed that the academic dean at the school was at odds with President Crawford and wanted to get rid of him. During an interview, the dean told the committee that nothing could be further from the truth, that he and Crawford got along very well, and he had nothing but respect for the man. Another asserted—it could not be confirmed by the committee—that Dr. Crawford had refused to move out of the president's campus home after his forced resignation (Jennifer Wiles, "The Drury Story," 4).

The Drury search committee, with one exception, recommended hiring Crawford as the college's new president. Although he had not been its first choice—several other candidates had declined the job offer—a sense that time was running out and the new school year was not that far away may have led the committee to seek quick closure. Speaking for the search committee, Judy Martin announced to the Drury community, "We felt Dr. Crawford had the skills to set Drury in the right direction. We knew he had some problems, but were impressed with how he had overcome them." The majority of the search committee members felt Crawford could serve as a peacemaker with the faculty, whose morale had bottomed out during the Bartholomy administration. "Although he had no fund-raising experience, we believed he would learn and develop" that talent.

An official at Salisbury State told the *Springfield Leader and Press* that at Salisbury, Crawford had "earned the love and respect of faculty and students for attracting top-notch professors and tripling the enrollment during his tenure." On February 26, 1981, Don Martin, the board member who chaired the search committee, offered a motion for the election of Crawford as president. The board approved and offered Crawford a one-year contract effective March 16.

Soon after his arrival on campus, Crawford found out that Drury's biggest problem was that the faculty was in litigation with the trustees over collective bargaining. Once he became familiar with the divisions, Crawford "felt like a physician who had been sent in to diagnose a patient" (*Springfield Daily News*, May 6, 1983). Tensions about unionization, as noted earlier, had polarized the faculty, and Crawford inherited the bitter acrimony still present between pro- and antiunion factions. Moreover, many faculty members believed Padron had unfairly been passed over for the job.

Six to nine months after arriving on campus, Crawford learned the board had elected him by a slim seven to six vote. "I didn't have the board's full support [for my appointment], which created a huge rift among board members" (Wiles, 3). He added, "There was significant resistance among the Board of Trustees to hire someone from the outside as president, and some were strongly supporting Dr. Padron's candidacy" (Wiles, 2). Moreover, the board had reneged on paying for his membership in a country club and procuring a new Cadillac for him. While these perks were not that important to him, he saw the fact that he never received them as a signal that he was not supported. As Steve Good, whom Crawford appointed as academic dean, observed, "A college president has a lot of difficulty if the board doesn't trust him."

Despite the rocky start, Crawford initially calmed things down with the faculty; the unionization battle ended. Julie Guillebeau, former head of public relations, believes that "he made it so it wasn't an issue, and it was resolved very quickly when the new administration moved in." Dr. Victor Agruso, then chair of the behavioral science department, remembers "most of the faculty initially supported Dr. Crawford. We collaborated for the good of the college." History professor James Smith called Crawford "the most capable, most compassionate, hardest working, open and honest administrator the college has had during his [Smith's] tenure." Judy Martin said he was kind to the faculty and related well to them: "They had lost their respect under Bartholomy, but Dr. Crawford helped build it back. He really listened to them and tried to see their point of view."

The day Crawford was hired, he announced his intentions of moving back into the president's house with his family, a decision applauded by all campus constituencies. "It was done because we [he and his wife, Garnette] wanted to, not for political reasons. We had always lived on campus at the other schools and really enjoyed being around the students on campus." The Crawfords decided to return the proceeds from the sale of President Bartholomy's off-campus home, asking that the funds be used for the renovation of the Benton Avenue structure, which needed a lot of work.

Crawford also got off to an extremely tenuous start with the students, according to Karen Sweeney. "He hadn't been at Drury for more than forty-eight hours when he went to a KA party and lost his keys." It wasn't long after that rumors began circulating not only on campus, but around town as well, "that he'd gone to the party, gotten drunk, lost his keys, and had to be taken home." Despite the fact that no such thing had happened, the story kept getting dredged up; efforts to set the record straight failed. Crawford recalled that there was even a phantom letter writer called Deep Purple who tacked rumors about the Crawfords on bulletin boards all over campus. Agruso observed that Drury students immediately began asking questions as to what the college president should and should not be doing without knowing the full story. "Students may want faculty and administrators to be their friends, but they don't want them to be students" (Wiles, 8–9). On the other hand, Crawford, who was comfortable interacting informally, believed he and his wife had a good relationship with students, and thoroughly enjoyed them despite the rumors. "We never missed an invitation to attend Greek events and the parties, especially the KA parties" (Wiles, 8).

At its annual Executive Council meeting of May 7, 1982, the board agreed to draft a new one-year contract for Crawford. At its regular meeting the following day, Crawford reported it had been a demanding year for him and that communications may have fallen short. He encouraged the board to call him in the coming year with any questions it might have.

Shortly thereafter Crawford's position precipitously declined. A student letter appearing in the October 8 *Mirror* asked:

> What is happening to Drury College? A few years ago, I was recruited to attend Drury, a college with a reputation for quality education. As an upper classman, I am seriously beginning to doubt this reputation. Undercurrents are strong at Drury now; and I feel I am being carried away by the undertow.

The letter caused quite a stir among students, faculty, and the administration. It went on to raise questions about the resignations of Dr. Flikkema as admissions director, followed within two days by that of Vice President for Academic Affairs Jorge Padron, who agreed to stay on until his replacement was found. And what of the transfer of Annette Avery, director of financial aid, to the Continuing Education Division? The letter complained about class scheduling that led to day students having to take many of their classes in the evening, and asked whether Drury was a day or night school. It demanded justification for the steady tuition increases and an explanation as to where the additional student fees went.

Partly in response to the letter, President Crawford decided to attend a Student Senate meeting called on October 12, 1982, to investigate "The Drury Rumor Mill." There he confirmed he had earlier asked Flikkema to leave his post as admissions director and return to the classroom, but denied responsibility for the transfer of Avery. He proposed that committees be formed to look into the problems at Drury and that "the solution is working together." He added that the overall atmosphere at Drury was gloomy: "The faculty was split, and the students were unhappy" (*Drury Mirror*, October 22, 1982).

More fuel was thrown on the fire when Jack Steck, the Panthers' nationally renowned swimming coach, quit after fourteen years at the helm over his perception that Crawford lacked the commitment to remedy the poor conditions of the Atha pool. "We just have to do something now or the swimming program at Drury can no longer exist. The pool is dirty, has only five lanes and a one-meter diving board" (*Drury Mirror*, February 4, 1983). Conditions had so deteriorated, he said, that Drury divers were forced to swim at SMSU, and other schools refused to compete at Drury. On the heels of Steck's departure, Springfield radio station KTTS broadcast an editorial claiming that Drury's president was involved in a behind-the-scenes power struggle, that he was inept at fund-raising, and that there were problems in the admissions office. Ominously, it mentioned that "Several colleges have gone out of existence, and others are sure to follow." It alleged that several well-known faculty members had resigned, and there seemed to be a general lack of confidence in the president, coming from at least half the faculty. In the author's opinion, clearly there were outside forces working to undermine Crawford publicly.

Because of federal and state budget cuts to higher education, Drury raised its tuition and room and board fees in both 1981 and 1982. A March 1982 audit particularly criticized the management of financial aid, leading to the aforementioned transfer of Avery. In November 1982, Gordon H. Howatt, Jr., who had worked with Crawford at Salisbury State, became Drury's vice president for business and management. The next month, he reported the budget for 1982–1983 was short by $340,000, and shortly thereafter announced Drury's third consecutive tuition hike. Meanwhile, under the stewardship of Dan Baker, the new admissions director hired to replace Flikkema, the number of students enrolled at Drury dropped dramatically. Twenty percent of the student population had not returned for the 1982 fall semester. In the spring of 1983, the admissions office reported that Drury had received 16 percent fewer applications than a year earlier. Indeed, under Crawford's tenure at Drury, the *Springfield Leader and Press* reported that total enrollment had slipped by 8.6 percent (April 24, 1983).

To compound the problems, Turner, Wallace, and Burnham halls needed more than $1 million in improvements. High energy costs, triggered by a rise in natural gas prices, added to Drury's financial woes. Faculty salaries remained low, falling even farther behind the inflation rate. There was talk of the need to reduce the number of scholarships for Drury students. Another source of contention was Crawford's conviction that student scholarships should be need-based, which was more characteristic of Eastern schools he was familiar with; he thought Drury ought to follow that model. However, that approach vied with the long-held notion at Drury of primarily offering scholarships to students on the basis of academic merit.

"The tension on campus was so thick you could cut it with a knife," said Victor Agruso. Everyone was fighting with one another. Many faculty developed health problems. Dean Sweeney said she cracked all eight of her back molars as a result of stress. "Judy Martin and I called each other every day just so we could tell each other we were normal and would survive," Sweeney recalls. "But the administrative team was loyal to Dr. Crawford, unfalteringly loyal."

Student morale also had deteriorated. While KULR was riding high, a result of its move to the Findlay Student Center, problems had occurred with the *Sou'wester*, when members of the staff took pay totaling nearly $1,000 in student fees after turning in only sixteen pages of copy. The publication's faculty advisor, Dr. Jay Bynum, completed the remaining 192 pages, and wrote on the closing page, "If I had had the power, I would have fired three of the last four editors and the head photographer" (*Drury Mirror*, October 23, 1981).

About a month earlier, the Alumni Council announced it would no longer sponsor Homecoming, citing scheduling problems, low attendance, and poor weather as its rationale. It would instead focus on Commencement weekend, combining those festivities with Homecoming and the class reunion weekend. The Student Union Board, aware of student disappointment about the decision, decided to sponsor Homecoming. The Opinions column of the *Mirror* lamented in its October 30, 1981, editorial that only two letters to the editor had been sent that fall, that Student Senate meetings on average lasted ten minutes, and that many student-faculty committees did not have enough students signed up to fill them. It berated those students who complained about everything, ranging from campus food described in colorful four-letter words, to maintenance so poor that they expected the campus to fall apart completely by 1999, to the pitfalls of the new plus and minus grading system.

The minutes of the April 25, 1983, meeting of the executive committee of the Board of Trustees reported that Drury was in "severe financial turmoil" (Wiles, 20). That conclusion and the decline of campus morale noted above formed the backdrop to the decision to ask for President Crawford's resignation, made at the April 29 board meeting. The chairman and vice chairman of the board announced they would not seek reelection. Board member Wally Springer presented a resolution that Dean Good be elected interim president beginning June 1, 1983. Good remained at that post until October 1983. Crawford, who was not present at the meeting, later opposed the resolution and felt he should be retained until the next president was hired.

What precipitated the end of the Crawford presidency? Certainly the uneasy, if not adversarial, relationship with the board played a part. His lack of fund-raising success also contributed. By the time Crawford resigned, the college debt totaled $1.2 million. Crawford "didn't see fund-raising as my principal job. Education was the most important thing to me. I wasn't trained or interested in being a fund-raiser. Instead, I wanted to maximize the opportunities for students and faculty to learn." His critics construed his laid-back style as an inability to make decisions, or, more amorphously, that he "wasn't presidential." Some questioned his communication skills and lack of political savvy. Perhaps, noted others, his previous experience, exclusively in public institutions, did not readily transfer to a private setting. Not helping matters was the unwillingness of the North Central Association (NCA), during its 1981 visit to campus, to sign off unconditionally on Drury's application for its ten-year reaccreditation. It called for a return visit in 1985–1986 to review the progress Drury had made in areas the NCA found deficient. (After the return visit, the NCA granted full accreditation without further stipulations.)

Likely all of these factors led to the conclusion that whatever Crawford's strengths as a person—kindness, candor, integrity—he was not the effective leader Drury needed. Perhaps Karen Sweeney best sums up the Crawford presidency: "There was a lot of suspicion and mystery pertaining to what a president would and could do. I'm not sure if Jesus Christ himself would have succeeded during these years at Drury." Professor John Simmons, president of the Drury chapter of the AAUP, referred to Crawford as being done in by forces beyond his control: "I am sorry he is leaving. I think he did a good job under difficult circumstances."

It was not easy for Crawford to leave Drury. "I felt I was letting a lot of people down, and even though I'd made reasonable progress, I left the job undone. I felt like I was a quitter. I just couldn't identify where the problems were coming from. And when I left Drury, it was headed toward real financial problems. I didn't feel good about that."

After leaving Drury, Crawford returned to Salisbury, Maryland, and stayed until he was offered a job at Delaware Community College. He next served as senior vice president at Townsend College in Washington, D.C., where he remained until 1987. That year he left to serve as interim president of a college in Maine. His last post was as vice president for public affairs at Thomas Edison College in Trenton, New

Jersey. At the time of this writing, Crawford was retired and living with his wife in Berlin, Maryland.

Neither Bartholomy nor Crawford had proved to be the knight in shining armor coming to the rescue of a Drury College in distress. Perhaps many hoped the third try would prove the charm; but as we shall see, rather than a knight, it was a mail-order bride who arrived on campus.

# Chapter 3

## Men for All Seasons: John Moore and Steve Good

John Moore and Steve Good came to Drury at virtually the same time. Both men made their mark on the school, individually and as a team—Drury's very own dynamic duo. If not miracle workers, they were the next best things. Both men were workaholics, although they might not accept that label, as they considered their work at Drury less a job than a calling. Their respect for each other was mutual and grew over the years. They played indispensable roles in the successes Drury enjoyed after 1983.

### The Mail-Order Bride

At a small university such as Drury, where the number of employees and students is relatively small and interaction among them frequent, the role of the college president is crucial. Not only is the president responsible for the financial well-being of the institution, mainly by fund-raising, but as chief executive he must set the tone for the school by listening to and showing respect for a diversity of viewpoints so different constituencies can work together. He needs to be sensitive to the different communication styles of trustees, faculty, and staff to avoid misunderstanding and divisiveness. He has to know how to lead but not to dictate, sensing when to intervene and when to step back. And according to Trustee Tom Kellogg, the president must be "committed to success and not afraid to tackle what success might require."

*John E. Moore, Jr., the fourteenth president of Drury (1983–2005), talks with students*

John E. Moore, Jr., Drury's fourteenth president, possessed those kinds of leadership skills in abundance. He had a firm grasp of what was going on in all areas of the college, from its day-to-day happenings to where he wanted Drury to be five or ten years down the line. At faculty meetings he employed an informal, folksy style of speaking, not hesitating to poke fun at himself, and usually spinning an interesting and humorous yarn or two. It was almost as if he and the audience were conversing at a coffee shop, or perhaps more accurately, were a bunch of "good old boys (and girls)" gathering at the general store to chew the fat. John Moore was adept at turning the spotlight away from his accomplishments, making sure to give credit to faculty, staff, trustees, and others for all the good things that were happening at Drury. But make no mistake about it: Despite the light, avuncular touch, Moore was clearly in charge. He could rattle off names and dates and, most impressively, connect a multitude of seemingly trivial matters to his larger vision of the university, both short-term and years down the road. To label John Moore a visionary is not to engage in hyperbole.

Despite Moore's multiple talents, he was a remote prospect when the presidential search committee began its deliberations in 1983 on the more than one hundred applicants for the position. His résumé fell short in the two areas the committee deemed essential for President Crawford's successor: college experience and a proven record in private fund-raising. Consequently, the presidential search committee initially put his application aside. Moore had served as assistant commissioner under Missouri Commissioner of Education Arthur Mallory, and when the committee notified Mallory of that decision, Mallory, who had been among those promoting Moore's candidacy, chided the committee. He assured them, according to Trustee John Hulston, "that John Moore could raise all sorts of money." Mallory praised Moore's exceptional communication skill and experience in handling budgets. Shortly thereafter, search team member Bill Harding, Drury's athletic director, was asked to visit the area where Moore had grown up and to inquire of the residents what they thought of the man. While there he visited with Mallory's father and Buffalo, Missouri, residents, from whom he heard nothing but the highest compliments about their neighbor. Harding, also a longtime Ozarks native, came back to the committee and said, "You know, we ought to take a look at this guy."

Meanwhile, Trustee Dr. Loren Broaddus had virtually become chair of the search committee while the official chair Dr. Claudine Cox was abroad and Ormal Creech, another veteran trustee, was recovering from surgery. Broaddus "was the only one left standing," as he jokingly put it. As the in-person interviews of the job finalists proceeded, Moore's candidacy came to look better and better to Broaddus, enough so that he went to the executive committee of the board to seek its approval for offering Moore the job. At the meeting, Trustee Mary Jane Pool delivered a rousing speech exalting Moore's stellar academic credentials.

*Robert Breech*

*Loren Broaddus*

*Mary Jane Pool*

*Wallace Springer*

On the eve of that meeting, Board of Trustees cochair Bob Breech had arrived in Springfield. He, Broaddus, and Wally Springer, the board's other cochair, who had been instrumental in guiding the search committee's work, went to dinner at the Steak and Ale, a local restaurant. Gathered there in a private room were a number of Missouri state legislators who, upon spotting Moore, jumped up, ran over, and greeted him effusively. Bob Breech recalled the outpouring of affection. When it came time for Moore to be introduced to the entire board, after a considerable wait in Dean Sweeney's office, Dr. Broaddus recounts that it was like a duck taking to water as Moore walked over to greet his new employers, asking about their families and sharing stories as if he were an old friend come to catch up on the latest news.

At the time he became Drury's president on October 13, 1983, the campus was in turmoil, experiencing serious budget deficits (around $1 million), declining enrollments, faculty conflict, administrative instability, and trustee dissatisfaction. As one faculty member recalls, "There was no laughter on campus." Moore says he knew there had been challenges and instability in leadership, and negative reports in the press for several years, some questioning whether Drury was resilient enough to make it. "But I didn't ask anybody to tell me all about the issues, the troubles, the problems that Drury had had. I guess I started with the view that, hey, we've got to build on the strengths. We have to take inventory of the pluses about this place. Then we can figure out where we go from there and build on those strengths, rather than dwell on where the weaknesses might be." In 1990, an Associated Press report ran the headline "Private Liberal Arts Colleges May Be Nearing Extinction." By that time, the *Drury Mirror* in good faith could retort, "Drury Not on Endangered College List," a status due in no small part to the work of John Moore (September 2, 1990).

On Thursday, October 25, a faculty music recital in Clara Thompson Hall served as the prelude to the inauguration of Drury's fourteenth president, scheduled for Saturday. The inaugural events consisted of a buffet luncheon from noon to 1:30 p.m. at the Findlay Student Center; the inauguration itself at 2 p.m. in Stone Chapel; a 3 p.m. reception at Walker Library, hosted by the Drury Women's Auxiliary; and lastly, the inauguration celebration running from 8 p.m. to midnight in the ballroom of the nearby Shrine Mosque, sometimes home to rock concerts and professional wrestling. Moore likes to say the schedule allowed him the chance to attend a school swim meet between the reception and the inaugural celebration.

Why did John Moore apply for the job at Drury and leave his important post in Jefferson City? Homesickness was one consideration for the Aurora-born Missouri native; after eight years away, he says that he was ready to return home. Ambition harnessed to service in higher education was another inducement: "I was looking for an opportunity to be captain of my own ship. I knew if all went well, you could cast a long shadow and have a lot of influence."

When Moore met the faculty for the first time in the Lay Hall Auditorium—his selection by the presidential search committee of trustees, faculty, and students had remained under wraps—most in the audience were clueless about the man poised to address them. President Moore's first words to the anxious audience were, "I feel like a mail-order bride who has just been delivered." The broad smiles that erupted and the hearty laughter that reverberated throughout Lay Hall augured a new, lighter mood on campus and the imminent return of optimism. Having won over the onlookers, Moore pledged to build on Drury's longstanding reputation and its strengths, above all conveying his confidence in the faculty, and his belief that by working together, they would turn Drury around. The audience disbanded feeling buoyed, not because the speaker glossed over the school's current problems and the long, hard work needed to fix them, but because he left them again feeling hopeful about the future of the school.

Moore was determined from day one that Drury get in the black and remain there. Karen Sweeney, thirty-one-year veteran and newly appointed executive vice president to President Moore, remembers him "running lean and mean, very frugal, personally and professionally." But turning Drury around would not occur overnight, as he inherited the accumulated baggage of almost seven lean years. Between 1974 and 1976, enrollments had declined from 949 to 824. The *Mirror* editorial of September 20, 1976, attributed the falling numbers to high tuition, insufficient specialized courses, and lack of weekend activities, resulting in student boredom. During the first four years of the Moore era, the head count hit 985, hardly a dramatic upswing. It wasn't until the fall of 1987 that enrollment began to take off, jumping to 1,042. As Table 1 below shows, the numbers continued to fluctuate over the next several years until the huge jump to 1,325 in 1996. Since 1998, enrollment has increased every year, setting all-time records each time. The numbers surpassed 1,500 in 2003, and by 2006 reached 1,612. Much of the credit for the upswing belonged to new Admissions Director Michael Thomas and his team, appointed in 1985 by President Moore.

*Drury administrators (l–r) Stephen Good, Judy Martin, President Moore, Karen Sweeney, and Jim Buchholz ca. 1999, before one of their annual fact-finding trips to another campus*

*Table 1: Day School Undergraduate Enrollment, 1983–2006\**

| YEAR | ENROLLMENT | YEAR | ENROLLMENT |
|---|---|---|---|
| Fall 1983 | 954 | Fall 1995 | 1,099 |
| Fall 1984 | 956 | Fall 1996 | 1,325 |
| Fall 1985 | 956 | Fall 1997 | 1,236 |
| Fall 1986 | 985 | Fall 1998 | 1,351 |
| Fall 1987 | 1,042 | Fall 1999 | 1,388 |
| Fall 1988 | 1,138 | Fall 2000 | 1,442 |
| Fall 1989 | 1,125 | Fall 2001 | 1,450 |
| Fall 1990 | 1,130 | Fall 2002 | 1,494 |
| Fall 1991 | 1,161 | Fall 2003 | 1,541 |
| Fall 1992 | 1,083 | Fall 2004 | 1,561 |
| Fall 1993 | 1,113 | Fall 2005 | 1,573 |
| Fall 1994 | 1,148 | Fall 2006 | 1,612 |

*\*Figures for the spring are always lower because of attrition. Note also there have been nine consecutive years of growth, resulting in a gross increase of 376 students.*

What accounts for Moore's part in the transformation of Drury from an institution on the verge of shutting its doors into a highly visible member of the Associated New American Colleges and eventually into a university? One might say that he was the right man, at the right time, in the right place, but there is more to it than that. He was the first Drury president who was native to the Ozarks, having grown up in the town of Monett. "I can talk about Missouri and how the people in the Ozarks think and operate," he said. Moore fished on Flat Creek and hunted quail with his grandfather, enabling him to relate well to local fishermen, hunters, and other outdoorsmen. Responding to a faculty member's inquiry as to whether he could trade cows in Nixa, Moore said, "You know, I think I could." That Ozarkers considered Moore one of their own put him in good stead when soliciting support for Drury in the community.

But this Ozarks native could also change dialects to speak with Eastern intellectuals. The first in his family to go to college, Moore won a scholarship to Yale University, where he earned his bachelor's and master's degrees in history. Following a stint in the in the army as an artillery battery commander, in 1968 he entered Harvard, where he completed a doctorate in education. He then traveled abroad widely, holding teaching and school administration jobs, and also serving as vice president of Athens College in Greece. His excellent liberal arts education in the East, military service, and work experience abroad exposed him to the ethnic and cultural diversity in areas outside of the Midwest, allowing him to feel at home in the broader world of academia and business.

Moore described his leadership style as hands-on, but not micromanaging. He strove to find good people, gave them broad portfolios of responsibility and authority, and supported them in what they were doing. As Trustee Lyle Reed, who came to the board in 1996, put it, "He is collegial but presidential and has been able to differentiate efficiently among administrative matters, informational topics, and trustee responsibilities. As president he sees the big picture while grasping the details needed to achieve the objective."

Moore felt strongly that Drury should be a collegial, cooperative place where people enjoyed working and maintained a sense of community built on respect and good communication. He immersed himself in details, wanted to be kept up-to-date, and had high standards and expectations. "I may be somewhat exacting to work for, but at the same time I am supportive of what they [staff and faculty] are doing." Yet Moore found time to mingle with students who remarked, "I don't know of too many places where the President of the college would come in and eat breakfast with you and *know your name*" (*Drury Mirror*, March 18, 1988). Moore's remarkable ability to remember names was evident at the numerous school functions he hosted and attended such as meetings with alumni and potential student recruits.

His relationship with the Board of Trustees was one of transparency, keeping them regularly informed of campus happenings at official meetings and by monthly letters summarizing developments at Drury. He regularly sent the board articles pointing out the latest trends and problems facing higher education, enabling them to place the Drury situation in a broader context. Moore's correspondence with the board confirmed his ability to think long-term about what Drury needed to do to maintain its reputation for academic excellence and its financial stability, while remaining competitive with public and private institutions in the recruiting battles for students. Board member Bob Cox described Moore as open and frank with the trustees, encouraging discussions on the major issues affecting Drury. Though rare, there were occasions where Moore had conflicts with the board; in one instance, with an "important" trustee who, in Moore's opinion, appeared to burden the Drury staff with unreasonable bureaucratic demands. Moore stood his ground and clearly did not tell that trustee what he wanted to hear.

But Moore's usual *modus operandi* was not to display "any personal disappointments or slings he may suffer, which encourages a highly cooperative spirit among the board members themselves." Trustee Wally Grimm, who joined the board in 1985 and served as chair of the finance committee for fourteen of those years, believed that Dr. Moore's presidency would go down as one of the best of all times. "I liken him to a modern-day Jim Findlay. There is no doubt in my mind that Drury is what it is today because of John and his leadership."

### Mr. Moore's Neighborhood

This writer experienced an incident that captures the essence of Moore's stewardship. It occurred one weekend shortly after Moore's arrival on campus, when, as I was ambling to my office, I thought I saw in the distance someone looking remarkably like the new president picking up trash while walking toward Burnham Hall. Of course, it was he!

Moore's concern with the appearance of the Drury grounds extended to the area surrounding it. In an interview with *News-Leader* reporter Steve Koehler that appeared on November 30, 2003, Moore spoke of a time early in his presidency of taking a stroll on Central Avenue and continuing south toward Chestnut Expressway where he encountered abandoned houses, the burned-out remains of a church annex, and a shabby warehouse. He lamented that this run-down area was Drury's front door, the place where visitors received their first impression of the college. Moore vowed to change the off-putting landscape, and kept his promise.

John Moore's sensitivity to Drury's role in the greater community was evident in his handling of the purchase of the 115-year-old Washington Avenue Baptist Church that long served north Springfield's African-American community. When it became clear that Drury's new science building would infringe on the church's home, while at the same time Pastor Maurice Tate was seeking to accommodate the growing congregation the old building could no longer hold, Moore led the efforts to find the church a new home. Drury also bought another church nearby whose congregation wanted to move, helped them to find another site, and arranged a loan to support their new facility. Drury then traded their old church for the Washington Avenue facility, giving that congregation a new home as well.

*The relocated and restored Historic Washington Avenue Baptist Church, now the Drury Diversity Center*

Not only that, but Drury paid for the costs of moving the old building just north of its historical location using the original brick, stained glass, pews, doors, windows, and steeple. The rebuilt church became a diversity center for the community. Moore recognized from the very beginning that church members had a vested and legitimate interest in the outcome and: "The best kinds of deals are deals where everyone comes out ahead." As Reverend Tate put it, "There were so many parties involved, and we all came out happy. I talk to others about what Drury did and they can't believe it." The video documentary *History Reborn* engagingly captures the story of the partnership between Drury and these neighbors.

Moore's deft touch extended to defusing other confrontations with area residents caused by the school's expansion into the historic Midtown neighborhood resplendent with older, attractive homes. Bob Horton, president of the Midtown Neighborhood Association, told *News-Leader* reporter Steve Koehler, "There were some tough spots. We have so many institutional neighbors surrounding us that there's a fear of them expanding into us rather than the other way around." When, in 1997, Drury announced plans to build a $5.5 million residential campus between Lynn and Calhoun Streets and Robberson and Jefferson Avenues, an area zoned for single-family residential development, many residents were less than thrilled. Those concerns were assuaged somewhat by a ten-year partnership agreement signed in March 1999 between Drury and the Midtown Neighborhood Association to resolve future growing-pain conflict between the college and its neighbors.

Midtown residents especially worried that the details of Drury's expansion plans were unknown. Between 1990 and 2000, the neighborhood, which encompassed 324 historical structures, had seen sixteen structures torn down, nine so that Drury could expand (*Drury Mirror*, May 5, 2000). They also were concerned that part of the property Drury had acquired was to be used for fraternities, whose reputation for being good neighbors sometimes suffered, usually in the wake of parties. They were reassured about the former by Drury's long-term master plan that spelled out the specifics of future acquisitions and construction, and about the latter by plans to move the fraternities to College Park, as the new residential area was called, where they could be more closely monitored for compliance with the university's housing regulations. Midtown Neighborhood Association President Ken Williams ('70) called the plan a landmark event for the city, certainly for his neighborhood. Rusty Worley, former vice president for administration, agreed: "The agreement might not allow Drury to grow exactly as it wanted, but we thought it was a good compromise."

Today, most residents view the university—which designed its master plan with their interests in mind—as a good neighbor that met with them to assure that any additional expansion would be limited and not destructive of the neighborhood's integrity. Bob Dixon, a state representative from the area, said that despite not always seeing things the same, "Overall, we realized we were all in this together. We truly benefit from each other." President Moore's appreciation for neighborhood concerns and his willingness to compromise helped Drury avoid the eminent domain squabbles that strained relations between other Springfield higher-education institutions and their neighborhoods.

One of the most prominent Midtown area residents, whose home was located on the corner of Benton Avenue and Calhoun Street, was none other than John Moore. At the time of his arrival, the almost ninety-year-old presidential home stood in serious need of renovations. Thirteen years into his presidency, Moore finally "got around" to dealing with the structure's deficiencies by renovating the interior. Moore accounted for the delay in repairs by asserting that spending large sums of money on personal furnishings and redecorating should not be a high priority for college presidents. Predictably, given his penchant to assure quality in all campus structures, he made certain that the renovations to the president's home met the highest standards, the implementation of which was taxing on those involved in doing the work.

To encourage further the preservation of the Midtown neighborhood, in January 2004 Drury announced a new loan and incentive program to encourage the renovation and purchase of single-family, owner-occupied homes by its employees. Participating employees would receive a 1.5 percent discount on home mortgages and improvement loans for the first five years of the loan, the subsidized lower rate to be split between Southwest Teachers Credit Union and Drury. Rusty Worley, who lived across from campus, urged faculty and staff to recognize that Midtown was a great neighborhood to live in, specifically the area bounded by Chestnut Expressway, Locust Street, and Sherman Avenue. Many Drury faculty and staff were already long-term neighborhood residents. On February 21, 2004, Mark Wood, chair of the chemistry department, his wife, Marie, and their son became the first Drury people to purchase a new home under the plan. Their new quarters, on the former site of Drury's Kappa Alpha fraternity house, were designed and built from scratch in a style harmonizing with the 150-year-old surrounding homes.

***

On May 4, 2004, Drury entered into a partnership with the Springfield School District to renovate and share the use of Harrison Stadium, constructed in 1936 as Senior High Stadium, and located at the intersection of Clay and Central streets. The project was hardly the first between Drury and the school district. In 1986, Drury and Springfield Public Schools jointly sponsored Summerscape, a program for gifted students, grades six through nine, and a few years later Summer Quest, for prekindergartners through grade five. Under the terms of the new agreement, Drury would pay for the construction of regulation football and soccer fields, as well as a 400-meter track. The school district would continue to use the revamped stadium for Pipkin Junior High and Central High football games and track meets, and for Central's Kiltie marching band and cheerleading rehearsals. President Moore expected to raise funds for the project, about $1 million, from outside donors. For its contribution, Drury would get to use the new field for home soccer games, track events and practices, intramural events, and campus gatherings. Once again, the Moore touch came up with a project that combined philanthropy and self-interest, private and public service. In the words of Dr. Michael Hoeman, school board president, "It comes at no cost to the taxpayers and is an example of a partnership that enhances programs at both schools while our community gets the most value from the district's budget." In August 2005, the green carpet of Harrison Stadium was afoot with players during the season openers for the men's and women's soccer teams.

*The renovated Harrison Stadium*

Moore's résumé clearly conveys how important community and civic participation are to him. From 1987 to 1990, he held the office of director of the Springfield Area Chamber of Commerce. From 1988 to 1989, he chaired the Make-A-Wish Foundation of Missouri. Also during 1988, he served as director of the United Way of the Ozarks and as president of the Rotary Club. Since 1999, he has headed the Board of Directors of the American National Fish and Wildlife Museum, and from 2002 has been a board member of the Upper White River Basin Foundation. Other examples of his civic and professional activities, past and present, include leadership and membership in the Ozark Council of Churches, the Community Relations Board of the Federal Medical Center, the Academy of Missouri Squires, the Missouri Colleges Fund, and the Greene County Financial Advisory Board.

In 1989, the Chamber of Commerce named Moore "Springfieldian of the Year." The man who nominated him, former Centerre Bank board chairman Ben Parnell, called him "a man for all seasons, who exemplifies the highest standards of leadership, both in his profession, and in his community and state." Philanthropist John Q. Hammons, unable to attend the banquet, appeared on a videotape message jesting that "John is aggressive, creative, and persistent. He's like a cold. You can't get rid of him." Neither Hammons nor any of the assembled guests suggested a cure for the common cold was imminent or, in this case, desirable. One year later the Springfield Contractors Association gave Moore the Developer of the Year Award. In 1993, he became a member of the Greater Ozarks Business Hall of Fame, and in 2001 his alma mater, Yale University, presented him with an award for "Recognition for Leadership in School Reform." On September 6, 2003, the Missourian Award, sponsored by the American Heart Association, acknowledged Moore as among the most accomplished citizens of the state of Missouri for his lifelong commitment to education and community service. They touted his leadership in transforming Drury from a small college into a university, setting a national example in areas such as science and mathematical literacy, university-school-community partnerships, and business education, and for helping students to make successful transitions to college. In all these endeavors, the sponsors recognized that Moore "has cultivated an atmosphere of collaboration and community."

The faculty got into the spirit of Moore appreciation by recognizing him for his twenty years of service at a meeting in the fall of 2003. He received from them a painting by local artist Jane Parker portraying his country cabin, "The Horse Creek Fish and Game Club," his place of respite and retreat. The artist drew the cabin from photos by economics professor and pilot Steve Mullins, who flew his plane over the site to shoot the pictures. On October 24, 2003, to mark Moore's twentieth anniversary as Drury's president, the Board of Trustees honored him by announcing the establishment of the John E. Moore Scholarship Fund, to which current and former trustees, families, and friends of the college donated more than $50,000. Board Chairman David Gohn offered these words of praise: "We on the board have been continually impressed with John's leadership and the progress Drury has made since he arrived in 1983. We are glad to be able to recognize his accomplishments." Deeply moved by two standing ovations, Moore responded: "It's rare for me to be rendered totally speechless, but you've done it. I am honored."

Moore's tangible contributions to Drury included fostering a rigorous academic program and a clear sense of mission, sustaining the health and strength of institutional finances, developing and maintaining campus facilities, and promoting higher levels of support from Drury's alumni and other friends. The less tangible ones involved restoring a sense of common purpose reflected in the collegial relations that pervade the Drury community, and inspiring a palpable spirit of forward momentum about the university and its future.

Given the enormous successes Moore had in rescuing Drury from the brink of disaster, and then developing it into a regional star, it is understandable that to a person the trustees interviewed for this book agreed that Drury's most difficult decision in the near future would selecting his successor, a sentiment shared by large numbers of faculty and staff. That decision would be made all the more difficult by the retirement of other long-term members of Moore's executive team such as Judy Martin and, as Trustee Virginia Bussey observed, "the task of replacing the multitude of excellent contributions of Provost Steve Good." Another friend of the university assessed the situation thusly: "All the decisions that have been made in the last ten years will pale into insignificance compared with that decision."

In April 2005, faculty and staff were invited to contribute to a video compilation of "farewell messages," a way of saying good-bye in their own personal ways to President Moore, who in 2004 had announced his plan to retire at the end of the academic year. On April 30 a "humongous" party was thrown by the faculty and staff at Trustee Science Center to express thanks to John Moore for twenty-two years of excellent leadership.

*The Man in the Bow Tie*

Stephen H. Good came to Drury in 1983 as dean and vice president for academic affairs. He earned a bachelor of arts degree from Nebraska Wesleyan University in 1964, a master's degree in English in 1965, and a doctor of philosophy in English and the history of science in 1972, both from the University of Pittsburgh. Prior to coming to Drury he was an assistant professor of English at Mount Saint Mary's College in Emmitsburg, Maryland, later becoming the department chair. He left in 1979 to become vice president and dean at Westmar College in Le Mars, Iowa. He told me that his undergraduate liberal arts education provided him opportunities to lunch with faculty from different disciplines and hear them talk about interesting ideas. This interaction fostered in Good a sense of just how positive an experience a small liberal arts institution such as Drury could be. Maintaining and enhancing that quality academic experience at Drury by emphasizing interdisciplinary learning became his mission. Perhaps an auspicious sign that this man would be right for Drury came at a presentation he made at the general faculty meeting shortly after being hired as the new dean. As Good was being introduced, Wayne Holmes, a crusty professor in the English department known for his directness, leaned over and said to Biology Professor Don Deeds and Communication Professor Charlie DeBerry, "He's kinda short, ain't he?" (Good stood roughly 5'4".) But as Good launched into his address, it became obvious to the many assembled that he already had a clear vision for Drury's future. The longer he spoke, the more impressed the faculty became. At some point Holmes leaned back over and whispered to Deeds and DeBerry, "You know, I think he's getting taller."

*Stephen H. Good*

Good had urgent problems to address, for he had walked into a maelstrom when he arrived on campus in 1983. The last two Drury presidents' controversial administrations had sharply sundered the faculty into supporters and detractors. Then in May 1983, President Norman Crawford resigned and Good became acting president of the college. (There is some evidence, suggestive but not conclusive, that Good harbored presidential ambitions at the time of Crawford's dismissal. Some years later he did apply for the presidency of a small liberal arts college, but subsequently withdrew his application.)

In his first meeting as acting president, Good recalled, "There had been an acrimonious effort to unionize. Ill will and backbiting created an environment that wasn't helpful and made it difficult to move on to other agendas." The rebuilding of harmony and the restoration of trust among faculty demanded top priority. To accomplish that end he promoted an agenda that physically brought the faculty together in a variety of settings. One such venue was the Friday faculty lunches; another was the holding of summer seminars inviting faculty from across the institution to break bread together and converse, and take part in mutual intellectual discourse. Along with his wife, Judy, he was an avid lover of campus theatre and musical events. He invited department chairs and other groups of faculty and their spouses to join him at performances preceded by a dinner in the Commons where the crowd could indulge in relaxed conversation.

To deal with declining enrollments, the acting president initiated a new financial aid program based on academic merit to make attending Drury easier for bright high school seniors. Good believed that the program was instrumental in raising enrollment. When the numbers came in better than expected that year, faculty received a small raise, which did much to boost their morale. All told, said Good, "Maybe we did a good job preparing the way for John Moore."

In 1989, with Good leading the way, the faculty and Board of Trustees refashioned the mission statement of the college. Its language renewed the continuing commitment to the liberal arts. It reads in part, "Education at Drury seeks to cultivate the spiritual sensitivities and imaginative faculties as well as ethical insight and critical thought; to foster the integration of theoretical and practical knowledge; and to liberate persons to participate responsibly in and to contribute to life in the global community." The new mission statement ensured that liberal arts knowledge and understanding remained central to the Drury Experience and fundamental to all its programs, including the new Global Perspectives 21 (GP21) curriculum.

Good cited the new mission statement, which he worked on prior to an accreditation visit by the North Central Association in 1990, as among his most gratifying accomplishments because it cogently articulated the overarching goals of a Drury education by integrating education theory with classroom practice. He also spoke warmly about the faculty's adoption of the GP21 curriculum and its science component, while downplaying his contribution, though in reality his encouragement and cajoling of the science faculty was instrumental in the new program's creation. That he selected these episodes was not accidental, for he was first and foremost a believer in and a theoretician of liberal arts education, and it was of the utmost importance to him that Drury define its mission with the liberal arts paradigm front and center. He also believed that a symbiotic relationship should exist between where Drury was going and the means for getting there. Certainly Good was not rigid in his conceptualization of the liberal arts, and exhibited pragmatism and a willingness to compromise to get GP21 approved. But flexibility and compromise did not require discarding the fundamental principles that he firmly believed were the essence of a liberal arts education.

Under Good's leadership, in 1995 Drury became part of a national consortium, the Associated New American Colleges (ANAC). At the time it consisted of five universities—now the number is much larger—representing the "peak of excellence," a term coined by Ernest Boyer, president of the Carnegie Foundation for the Advancement of Teaching. The consortium recognized colleges and universities combining aspects of the liberal arts college and the research university, institutions particularly effective in integrating professional preparation with the liberal arts. Most of today's ANAC colleges and universities are medium-sized, student populations numbering from 1,500 to 5,000, with predominantly undergraduate students. Typically these colleges have more resources than traditional liberal arts colleges, but are small enough to retain personalized education. Historically, ANAC schools have been interested in the examination of values, often in the context of a church relationship, helping students to recognize the value implications in all the academic disciplines as well as the professions.

A paper Good coauthored with President Moore and presented to ANAC stressed the value of the Drury education mix—a combination of professional programs and traditional liberal arts subjects. The paper's classification of Drury as a hybrid institution helped dissipate an ongoing dispute between purist and pragmatist faculty about the direction Drury was moving, and had a beneficial effect on campus morale.

Good further distinguished himself as an articulate spokesperson for ANAC and its model of integrated learning. Fellow member George Sims, vice president for academic affairs at Muskingum College, remarked, "In Steve's company we were more collaborative, more collegial, more open to new ideas, and more productive than we would have been without him." In 1994, the Council of Independent Colleges named Dean Good its Chief Academic Officer of the Year.

In a Founders' Day address delivered on September 23, 1999, entitled "The Idea of the University," Good foreshadowed the ensuing name change from Drury College to Drury University, which came to pass on January 1, 2000, three days after a vote by the Board of Trustees. Don Ameye, the graphic designer in the Public Relations office, designed the new Drury University image. His design incorporated a traditional typeface in a somewhat modern pattern. The word *Drury* is larger and more prominent than *University* to underscore the school's continuing commitment to the liberal arts, whereby it would remain a medium-sized institution where professional and liberal arts programs worked in tandem.

There were, of course, those who contended that the name change might not be good for the college, that it meant sacrificing or dramatically changing the tenor and mission of Drury. Most, however, felt that Drury University would remain on a humane scale and continue to honor the importance of small classes and a low student-faculty ratio. Most importantly, the "new" Drury University would continue to provide a very strong liberal arts context for the professional preparation of its students. In point of fact, the name change simply recognized what Drury College had in fact become over the years, rather than breaking new ground.

Good's management style derived from his genuinely liking all the people he worked with. He enjoyed engaging faculty in conversations about the university's broad goals and how he could help them contribute to realizing them. "We are a community of scholars committed to certain values: honesty and integrity, high expectations, democracy, truth and beauty. We care for and support our colleagues in the challenges they face." Good believed that generally faculty "want to do the right thing, and we are better served to support their interests and connect them to broader institutional goals than to try to dictate to faculty what they ought to be doing." While Good was passionate about issues, he learned early on that the dean has to moderate that intensity, for it can intimidate people. "One of the greatest joys for me has been working with the faculty. I could not have asked for a better group of colleagues and that really hasn't changed over the years."

That admiration was mutual, which is unusual, in that deans and faculty don't always—should I say "usually"?—like one another. But the Drury faculty honored Good on many occasions, including a surprise tribute at the annual Faculty Retirement Dinner held in May 2003 to mark his twentieth anniversary at Drury. The high point of the festivities was the announcement of the Stephen H. Good Scholarship for Academic Excellence. The scholarship recognizes outstanding student performance in the GP21 program, and supports study-abroad opportunities to fulfill the intent of the global studies curriculum. At the September opening convocation for the 2003–2004 academic year, Good's colleagues bestowed on him the Faculty Award for Academic Excellence. The citation for the award read, in part, "It is simply impossible to overestimate the positive impact of Dr. Good's academic leadership and personal dedication on the Drury community and all its members. His passion for liberal arts learning, his commitment to infusing professional programs with that passion, along with his personal warmth and unimpeachable integrity, have transformed this institution's educational programs. Dr. Good has defined what it means to be a member of the Drury community." At a roast that evening, Professors Roger Young (biology) and Lisa Esposito (philosophy and religion) toasted the dean by performing Young's lyrics, rap style, over the rhythm arranged by Professors Don Deeds (biology) and Chris Panza (philosophy and religion). The last stanza (the reader will have to imagine the syncopation) was:

> *He's the Drury man, he's front-page news*
> *Always looking good from his ties to his shoes*
> *The dean is here and shows leadership*
> *And you know he's a fighter and he'll never quit*
> *Drury is the place and Steve's the name*
> *He showed us guidance, and brought us the fame*
> *He's been there for all of us, he's the leader of our gang*
> *So put it together y'all, cuz ... Steve Good is ... the Man.*

When Good was diagnosed with melanoma in 1999, the outpouring of concern, love, and affection by the faculty, and for that matter, the entire Drury community, was overwhelming. What made it more incredible, according to Dale Simmons, Good's fellow provost and vice president for academic affairs at Judson College in Illinois, is that such tributes, while not uncommon to those who have been outstanding faculty members, take place rarely for administrators, "just by the virtue of the nature of our work."

When he went off to Houston, Texas, for surgery, Good was inundated with videos of numerous well-wishers, a signed blown-up photo of faculty and staff posed on the steps of Olin Library, myriad flowers, and countless messages offering prayers and heartfelt wishes for a speedy recovery. Despite that surgery and others that followed, and painful chemical treatments, after recuperating, Good always returned to his campus office, where he unflaggingly performed his duties, keeping to his usual routine despite his physical difficulties.

It was only in the last two months of his illness that he was unable to come to campus every day. Less then two weeks before he passed away on Monday, February 16, 2004, several faculty members visited him at home. One of them, Communication Professor Regina Waters, recounted "that he was in true Steve form—he took a break from reviewing tenure portfolios to chat with us for a while!" A memorial service was held on Thursday, February 19 at Wesley United Methodist Church, where an overflow crowd came to say their farewells to Drury's "little giant." On May 13, 2005, a freestanding bronze statue designed by James Hall, president of JH Creative, and given to the school by the senior class was dedicated to Drury's beloved provost. It depicted him seated on a bench outside of the Olin Library, a favorite place of his, reading a book and wearing his signature bow tie, and in the words of student Susie Schroer, assuring that his disarming smile "is everlasting on the Drury campus."

On March 8, 2004, the Drury Singers, the Drury Orchestra, the Drury Woodwind Quintet, the Drury Jazz Band, and the Drury Concert Band gave a memorial concert in Clara Thompson Hall celebrating Dr. Good's life and legacy. Concert highlights included Music Professor David Goza, alone on the stage with his oboe surrounded by four music stands, with his back to the audience. As the notes to the prelude of Vincent Perischetti's "Serenade No. 14, Opus 169" flowed out, Goza rotated counterclockwise to face each station, gyrating with his oboe in a captivating dance of commitment to the music as a metaphor for life. "We come from nothing and go back to nothing." Bow ties, Good's trademark fashion accessory, could be seen sprinkled throughout the audience. At intermission Judy, his widow, who along with her husband was a regular at the music department's concerts and recitals, was presented with a book of stories and recollections from the Drury community about her husband.

Student Kelly Foster recalled meeting Dean Good for the first time under "less than wonderful circumstances." He listened to her politely and reassured her. Thereafter, when they met on campus he would ask her how classes were going, and told her if she needed anything, to come see him. Shortly before her graduation in 2003 they ran into each other, and to his question about her plans after graduation, she replied that she was going to graduate school "so that I someday can come back to Drury as a professor." His response: "Great. Drury could use people like you." Foster earned her degree despite having cerebral palsy.

Music major Erica Spires remembers that when she interviewed Good for a newspaper, his first words—Spires is a talented singer—were, "I'm a big fan of yours." Subsequently, he attended almost all of her performances, "after which he proceeded to have a real conversation with me. I have never met someone outside of the music and theatre departments, especially a very busy administrator, who was so dedicated to supporting the arts." Art department chairman Tom Parker recounts that when returning late to campus from a conference, he called the dean—who seemed to be on campus by the crack of dawn—to get a message to his 8 a.m. art class that he would be late. When Tom, true to his promise, arrived forty-five minutes later, he had just enough time to catch the last part of Good's lecture on the artist Thomas Hogarth, replete with slides, pointers, and all the flourishes.

Creating and maintaining a supportive campus atmosphere is the legacy Steve Good left to Drury University. He asked faculty to become more engaged in the lives of their students, reminding them of the importance of time spent with students outside of the classroom. He fostered an environment that encouraged faculty to be scholars and mentors, as well as guardians of the institution. He was a wise counselor to faculty and students alike, pushing them to make the most of their time and Drury's resources, and reaffirming the high expectations Drury had of them.

In a poignant letter to the Drury community on February 18, 2004, President Moore spoke of Good's many remarkable accomplishments and "the wonderful relationship we had with him." Shortly before his death, Good told Moore how his life had been blessed, and how much his nearly twenty-one years at Drury had meant to him. Moore described him as the "dean's dean," keenly intelligent, a scholar, teacher, and friend. "He understood what a liberal arts education was all about and could articulate its shape and substance better than anyone I have ever known." Steve and Judy Good, together, in addition to attending virtually all cultural events on campus, were ardent Panthers athletic boosters, clapping and cheering on the men's and women's basketball teams—okay, let's face it, Judy was the more emotional fan, while Steve's less vocal show of support "never compromised his dignity."

*The Dynamic Duo*

At first look, John Moore and Steve Good appeared to be very different, both in physical appearance and personal demeanor. The key to the men's relationship was the mutual respect they had for each other. In his tribute to Steve Good, President Moore said, "We were close friends for more than twenty years, and although we were quite different in many ways, we were always remarkably close. We respected each other and acknowledged each other's strengths and complemented each other as members of Drury's administrative team. I always marveled at his remarkable abilities, and was never joking when I acknowledged him frequently as the 'brains of the operation.'" With Good pretty much running the academic side of things, Moore spent his time on working with the board, fund-raising, new construction, and long-term strategic planning; this division of labor redounded to the benefit of the college by efficiently and effectively harnessing the high energy and talents each man possessed.

About John Moore, Dean Good said, "We are good friends. We have a profound mutual respect. I think he was exactly the right person at the right time for the presidency here. Dr. Moore is a hunter, fisherman, and outdoorsman. So we don't share hobbies outside of work. But he has always respected and supported my work and largely let me provide leadership to the academic area of the institution. We shared our views candidly and never in twenty years have we gotten angry at one another. John is tremendously bright, thoughtful, and articulate." Their disagreements never became personal because they were issue-driven and defined in terms of what was best for the college. As Good said, "Decisions are taken and we move on."

As we have seen, Moore was easy to chat up, as he was most welcoming and informal in conversation. He was also a wonderful teller of stories, sometimes conveyed in colorful language, always recounted at a leisurely pace. These tales were a vital part of Moore's doing business "Ozarks style." Other winning qualities of Moore's are illustrated by an incident that took place in his executive assistant Pat Schreiner's reception area. I had seen him there on the way up to my office when he gestured to me to come in. We proceeded to engage in a lively discussion of some academic topic or other. While we were chatting away, a young faculty member dropped in to solicit the school president's help as to where he might hold a fly-casting clinic for interested faculty. Moore welcomed him, quickly shifted gears, and immediately offered the use of his cabin and pond to the group. This incident and others mentioned portray a multitalented president, who was readily accessible to all, willing to do trash removal, and comfortable in talking about both academic scholarship and the finer points of fly-casting.

Good appeared more formal and reserved, and was perceived by some as intimidating; that is, until they got to know him and his delightful sense of humor. There is a tradition at Drury where, after twenty-five years, faculty receive a plaque at graduation acknowledging their dedication and service to Drury. That somber occasion was nearly mortally wounded by the 1990 honoree Dr. Sidney Vise, who when Dean Good called his name, ran full speed down the aisle in regalia and made a grand leap onto the platform. Seizing the microphone, he exclaimed to a stunned Steve Good, whose reputation for unflappability was legendary, "Like far out man, super cool, thank you." The popular pianist then executed a virtuoso running leap off the platform. Vise, not normally known for such displays, later said, "I had the urge to shatter the image when my time came." When the more than two thousand assembled guests and graduates finally finished laughing, Good, who by then had recovered his composure and was not one to be outwitted, retorted deadpan, "And our faculty are never lacking in dignity" (*Drury Lane,* September 1999).

When Jeff VanDenBerg, the current chair of the history and political science department, was invited in his first year at Drury to accompany the dean to a Council of Independent Colleges conference in St. Louis, his neophyte nerves, combined with Good's reputation for high expectations of Drury faculty conference participants, put him on edge. By conference end, following a jog around the Arch to which Good invited him, and during which they chatted about family, sports, travel, and politics—missing a conference session while they ran!—VanDenBerg felt he had bonded with the dean.

When faculty visited with Good in his cozy office, they sat near the fireplace in comfortable chairs arranged to invite closeness. Following some small talk, the visitor was encouraged to proceed fairly quickly to the matter at hand, while Good listened very carefully to what he or she had to say. He had the knack of making the visitor feel not only that he was providing his undivided attention, but also that what the speaker was saying was of incredible importance to him. Good could make a dissenting point, yet do so with the most amazing tact, skill, and grace. His replies were always thoughtful, almost delivered like a flawless essay, presented in such a logical and orderly manner that after interviews for this book there was virtually no need to do any tinkering with his comments to put them in written form.

The teamwork of Moore and Good improved Drury on all levels, resulting in an exciting new curriculum, strengthened academic programs, and numerous community service and student life programs for an increasingly diversified student body.

# Chapter 4

## The Drury Difference

### *The New Adventure Begins*

In 1983, Drury began its climb to national recognition with its appearance in *Peterson's Comprehensive Guide to Colleges and Universities,* a well-respected publication consulted by prospective college students and their high school counselors. By 2000, the prestigious *U.S. News and World Report* college guide ranked Drury number one on its list of the Midwest's "Great Schools at Great Prices," a position sustained through 2002; for 2003, 2004, and 2006, the numbers were two, four, and three respectively. The same publication ranked Drury twelfth among its noteworthy Midwestern Master's Universities in 2003, tenth in 2005, and an all-time high of ninth in 2006. *Yahoo! Internet Life* cites Drury among its 50 Most Wired Small Colleges, and in 2005 and 2006, the *Princeton Review* referred to the school as "small but mighty," and a Best Midwestern College. While the rankings need to be taken with a grain of salt, they do suggest that the institution is doing many things right in providing a quality educational experience, and they broaden national awareness of the school's strengths. What accounts for the many accolades Drury has accrued over these two decades?

Certainly among the relevant factors are Drury's Global Perspectives 21 curriculum, its distinguished faculty (more than 90 percent hold a doctorate or the highest degree in their field), and its nationally recognized orientation program for new students. At the opening of the 2003–2004 academic year the Drury undergraduate student body numbered roughly 1,500 (55 percent women and 45 percent men), and they presented entering test scores averaging 25-plus on the ACT, a national exam taken by high schoolers seeking admission to colleges and universities. Sixty-three percent were in the top 25 percent of their high school graduating class and earned an average high school grade point average (GPA) of 3.6 on a 4.0 scale. They represented thirty-seven states and fifty-one nations. Fifty percent lived on campus.

In Springfield, Missouri, many locals regard Drury as a rich kids' school based on their perception of the family income of attending students. That perception is not accurate. More than 80 percent of Drury students receive financial aid, based on need and scholarship. The average financial aid package totals around $5,200, a figure that does not include state or federal loans and grants. Most Drury students work part-time to help pay for their educational expenses; few leave the university debt-free.

Nor is it the case that Drury students are ruthlessly competitive. Susan West ('75) commented in a 1990 *Drury Lane* interview, "I'm not saying that students are coddled at Drury, but we were never exposed to the nasty, competitive atmosphere that exists in the real world. At Drury there was more of a universal quest for knowledge, with students cooperating and helping each other." Drury, continued West, who graduated with a double major in biology and chemistry, was unlike other schools, where "students were just as likely to spit in each other's test tubes as anything else."

Randy Eaton, former president of the Alumni Council, described the Drury community as a collection of "many different backgrounds and attitudes." He remembers with special fondness Professor Edythe West. "She was sure to bring out the best or worst in you," Eaton recalls. "She thought many of the students were spoiled and pretty self-centered. She made sure we understood that the world was not exactly what our comfortable lives were all about."

Mindy Buckner ('99) perceived the Drury environment as intriguing and friendly. She singled out Chip Parker from the admissions office for helping her feel comfortable. "He was very friendly and answered all my questions and concerns about Drury," she remembers. "Because of his willingness to help, it made me realize that the faculty would be just as willing to help me once I was a student." In the spring of 2004, that very same Chip Parker received the Peggy Clinton Memorial Award from the Missouri Association for College Admissions Counseling (MOACAC) for his dedication and commitment to this organization and the recruiting profession in general.

Rodrigo Pantoja said he was looking for a school that was not very large, where individuals count in the decisions of the university, and a place where students were intellectually challenged by their professors. "I was looking for a university where people care about their students," he added.

Katy Richardson, a Drury senior in 2004, thought that Drury could be improved by having students interact more outside of the community: "Sometimes we feel so at home here that we get sheltered into this little enclosed community. Everyone here is so friendly, and we do get treated wonderfully." Sadly, says Richardson, in the real world that would not always be the case.

Architecture major Marin Pastar, who came to Drury from Sweden, lived with President John Moore and his wife, Joann, during his four years at Drury. His host family in Springfield set up a meeting at the Moore home, and he was astonished when the Moores, after talking with him for about five minutes, invited him to reside with them. "They have become like a family away from home," Pastar said.

Nohora Cardenas was active in the Drury Friends Program, which paired up an international student with an American so they could get to know each other better. Her most memorable moment was organizing the first International Student Association (ISA) dinner, at which international students provided cuisine and entertainment for the American guests. The event allowed people from different cultures on campus to meet and interact. Cardenas described Drury as a very friendly place and praised the closeness between students and professors, while calling for more diversity on campus.

The Drury Experience also brought accolades from families who had several members, or even several generations, receive a Drury education. Joyce Pyle's father, Professor Oscar Fryer, taught physics at Drury from the 1930s through 1967. She remembered playing in Pearsons Hall from the time she was three years old. She said that Drury never strayed from its mission of stimulating the students' thinking. "We either had to come up with new beliefs or defend rationally what we believed," she remembers.

Her husband, Bill, also graduated from Drury. He recollected working at awful jobs after three years in the army, and remains grateful for being accepted to Drury with very few credentials. "I would say that Drury went beyond my expectations. It helped me become a happier person." Both of their daughters graduated from Drury, as did their two sons-in-law.

The author remembers well the first time he experienced the "family connection" at Drury. Sometime around his thirtieth year at the school, while calling the names on the class roster, he remarked to a student on the list, "I had your brother as a student in this very same class." To his chagrin, the student sheepishly replied, "Do you mean my father?"

Student Audrey Campbell's story was similar to those of many others: "My sister was a biology major at Drury. She is living in Des Moines, Iowa, attending medical school there. She was the one that talked me into coming to Drury. She told me how Professor Don Deeds, who also graduated from Drury, was very influential in preparing her for medical school." Campbell, whose mother also attended Drury, interviewed Deeds for this book, and regretted not asking him more about what her sister was like in school: "Was she a nerd or did she hardly study at all?" Campbell wondered.

Paul McGowan, who followed his brother to Drury, met his wife-to-be Naomi during Freshman Orientation in June 1998 though they did not start dating until his junior year. Four months later they were engaged, and they married on June 8, 2002. "Naomi and I had a wonderful time at Drury," McGowan said. "We feel very blessed to have been able to be a part of Drury history, and we can't think of a better place to have met and fallen in love." One wonders if their son, Craig Matthew, will follow in his parents' footsteps by attending their alma mater. For the record, there are hundreds of "Drury Sweethearts," alumni couples who met at and graduated from Drury, some of whom were invited to tell their stories at a recent alumni reunion.

Jennifer Nelson, upon entering the Drury campus in the fall of 1999, fell in love with the atmosphere of the Drury community: "The students would say 'hi' to me if they met me on a sidewalk, or open doors for me as we explored the buildings." The beauty and upkeep of the campus, and the new plants lining the walkways, made Drury seem more like a town plaza than a college campus.

\*\*\*

First-year students undergo a four-day orientation before classes begin, involving team-building exercises, picnics, fireworks, other fun and bonding activities, as well as attending a dessert held in faculty and staff homes. They meet the other students in their Alpha Seminar (a yearlong class on the American experience required of all freshmen), and their Alpha mentor, the instructor who also serves as their academic advisor for the First-Year Experience. Shortly after arriving on campus, Alpha groups discuss a class reading mailed earlier. Hence before school officially begins, new Drury students have had the opportunity to become acquainted with the curriculum, meet the instructors, and perhaps most importantly, begin to make new friends.

Drury's program for first-year students, considered by *Time* magazine to be one of the best in the nation, represents the first indication to students of their new school's commitment to personalized education. The Policy Center on the First Year of College designated Drury, along with twelve other colleges and universities nationwide, an "Institution of Excellence in the First Year of College," praising Drury for effectively helping its students make a successful transition from high school to the academic demands of college. In 2006, the Association of American Colleges and Universities recognized the general education requirements for Drury undergraduates as a national model for incorporating international issues, local experiences, ethics, and science and math into the academic life of a university. Its report noted that "Drury University's core curriculum is an especially good example of the role that global learning goals can play by linking multiple elements of the curriculum." The National Survey of Student Engagement, which tracks how challenged college students are, based on surveys of 135,000-plus students at more than six hundred colleges and universities, placed Drury in the top 10 percent in the category of Academic Challenge, and awarded it a rating in the *one hundredth percentile* in the category of Active and Collaborative Learning.

*What I Study: Global Perspectives 21*

All college curricula have general requirements, classes in a variety of academic disciplines that students are required to take in addition to those courses mandated by their major field of study. Leafing through descriptions of these general education courses is not enticing for most readers, nor is rummaging through the hundreds of pages of committee minutes, single-spaced, that summarize the five years between the decision to write a new curriculum in the summer of 1990 and its implementation in August 1995. These caveats notwithstanding, I'll risk taking the reader through some of the high points of Global Perspectives 21.

The idea to redo the curriculum was the brainchild of Dean Steve Good. It went from him to the Educational Policy Committee, which has to approve new schoolwide courses; in turn, EPC proceeded to create numerous subcommittees (some claim the number approached infinity) to reevaluate the current academic subject areas, to design the new required core courses, and to integrate both of them into a cohesive structure that would answer the questions: What do we want our students to know, and what do the faculty want them to be able to do? From the committee deliberations over the next three years, three broad positions emerged: 1) Tinkering with the curriculum already in place was sufficient, 2) Scrapping pretty much all current required courses and replacing them with new ones was the only way to go, and 3) Coming up with a hybrid solution that avoided the conservatism of plan 1 and the radicalism of plan 2 was essential for obtaining faculty approval of any curriculum. (The faculty had earlier rejected a proposal adhering to approach 1.) Periodically Dean Good voiced concerns that the subcommittees not get ahead of the faculty in their deliberations, and instead stay focused on Drury's mission statement as the basis of their plans.

The reader should be aware that reforming a curriculum is not simply a question of the faculty exchanging sublime ideas in a vacuum sometimes called the ivory tower. For one thing, there are limited resources: finances, materials, and personnel. For another, most faculty expertise is discipline-specific. Was the Drury faculty willing or able, intentions aside, to venture into the *terra incognita* of interdisciplinary classes? If the answer was an enthusiastic yes, would there be enough faculty available to meet departmental duties and new Global Perspectives teaching responsibilities? If not, did that mean hiring additional faculty, and if so, was money available to do so? These kinds of practical concerns, when added to the ever-present content disagreements, help explain why at Drury and elsewhere major curriculum reforms take place infrequently, roughly once every generation (1894, 1910, 1941, 1978, 1995), using Thomas Jefferson's figure of eighteen years as a benchmark. (Jefferson, of course, suggested that revolution, not curricular reform, marked the arrival of the new generation, though the pain involved in shedding old curricula may not be dissimilar.)

*The Evening College, now called the College of Graduate and Continuing Studies, continues to serve thousands of adult and part-time students*

Dean Good was instrumental in procuring faculty assent that the goals of the revised curriculum would cultivate the abilities of students to think critically, communicate effectively, empathize, make mature value judgments, exhibit personal and social responsibility, and chart a healthy course for life. The reforms stressed that all Drury graduates be familiar with the Western tradition, including its history, its great ideas and significant artifacts, while providing students with opportunities for in-depth studies and tools for integrating theoretical and applied learning.

To create a model global community in which the best values of the liberal arts and the Judeo-Christian tradition governed, the new curriculum advocated a campus mindset that affirmed the equality and worth of all peoples by focusing upon the diversity of human culture, language, history, and values. It endorsed a gender-blind environment supportive of the development of the whole person: intellectually, socially, morally, emotionally, physically, and spiritually. It called for preparing Drury students for a time of significant global adjustment by strengthening their understanding of science and technology, their perception of the interrelatedness of all things, their appreciation of beauty in nature and the built world, and their love of truth and freedom.

The Global Perspectives 21 curriculum that finally emerged was academically rigorous and demanding. Most of the core courses were interdisciplinary in nature. To graduate, Drury students had to earn 124 credit hours; 57 to 60 of them (roughly 50 percent) were GP21 classes, a rather large number compared to the core curricula at most institutions of higher learning, and a continuing source of spirited debate among Drury faculty—some thought the prescribed courses cut into the hours needed for majors, others that the number was about right or erred on the low side. Despite some unhappiness with the details, the final approval by the faculty reflected a consensus that the liberal arts remain the centerpiece of the Drury learning experience, and that GP21 integrate with the major program of study.

*The Great Compromise*

The Alpha Seminar explores four themes: Community and the Individual, Identity and Difference, Private Interest and Public Welfare, and Life and Work. The process-oriented seminar utilizes a faculty-prepared interdisciplinary reader consisting mostly of primary sources, supplemented by other readings to investigate case studies of different topics within the American experience.

Concomitantly, students work toward completing the History of Western Culture requirement. This means selecting two courses, usually completed by the end of the sophomore year. One selection comes from courses engaging the Ideas and Events of Western Culture, whose objective is to develop a comprehensive understanding of broad periods in Western cultural history; the other from Artifacts of Western Culture, which covers literature and art relevant to Western history. Mostly as sophomores, Drury students enroll in Global Awareness and Cultural Diversity, where they examine and acquire skills for analyzing world cultures. They apply these skills in Minorities and Indigenous Cultures, where they choose a course that focuses intensely on a single world culture "conspicuously different" from that of the United States. During the sophomore and running into the junior year, they enroll in a Values Analysis class, where they apply various ethical approaches to different situations. In Global Futures, students look at trends and prospects from the perspective of responsible citizens of a global community, and pull together their knowledge and skills from GP21 courses taken earlier in the sequence. In addition to the Global Studies courses, students also have to satisfy GP21 distribution requirements in Scientific Perspectives, Creativity Explored, Human Behavior, Health and Well-Being, Political Science, or Economics. Lastly comes the capstone experience of a Senior Research Project or Seminar where they write papers that connect their Global Studies classes to their academic majors.

A Theme Year Convocation series complements GP21. Begun in the 2000–2001 academic year, this series replaced the program under the old curriculum, which consisted of weekly convocations featuring a plethora of speakers, many of them in-house, who spoke on a variety of interesting but not directly related topics. The Theme Year series, as the name indicates, selects a single subject to explore over the course of the year, and chooses its presenters accordingly. In consecutive order, the convocation series themes have been: "A Celebration of Diversity," "Origins," "Gender and Sexuality," "Creativity, Exploration, and Discovery," "For the Common Good: Private Interest and Global Citizenship," "Sustainability: Environmental, Cultural, and Economic," and "Liberty and Security in a Post-9/11 World." A brief list of convocation speakers reads like a Who's Who from the world of the arts and sciences: Sister Helen Prejean, Morris Dees, Oliver Sacks, Judy Chicago, Patricia Ireland, Brian Greene, Christina Hoff Summers, Eric Schlosser, Bruce Feiler, Rick Moody, and Barbara Ehrenreich. Convocations are generally open and free to the public. Speaker presentations are available online. To access them, go to the Drury Web site (www.drury.edu) and type "theme year" into the Search box.

In the fall of 1996, Drury introduced a new integrated mathematics and science curriculum required for all nonscience majors, with the goal of producing graduates who were literate in mathematics and science. The program evolved from the participation of Drury mathematics and science professors, as well as President Moore and Dean Good, at a 1992 meeting of Project Kaleidoscope (PKAL), an organization dedicated to the improvement of undergraduate math and science education. PKAL stressed the importance of maintaining both a first-rate science program and state-of-the-art facilities. In 1993, the Drury faculty approved an increase in science and mathematics requirements from nine to twelve hours. Next the Mathematics and Science Division of the college took on the task of developing new courses to fulfill the expanded requirements. Initially the group thought it would simply develop new introductory courses for each of the division's four departments: mathematics, biology, chemistry, and physics. When the group proudly presented the results of their deliberations to Good, they were taken aback by his response: "You have got to be kidding, right?"—referring to the proposal's lack of bold thinking. There followed the scheduling of a series of workshops over the next several years, in which the division unleashed its creative energies, in an atmosphere devoid of the usual turf wars over the importance of individual academic specialties. Indeed, to the surprise of most attending, the thrust of the deliberations centered on what the different sciences had in common, emphasizing the approach of each to a better understanding of the natural world.

Another significant outcome of the deliberations was the decision to seek funding from the National Science Foundation (NSF) Course and Curriculum Development program. The NSF agreed to fund the submitted proposal for two years beginning in May 1996, which led to a combined NSF/Drury matching grant of $216,000. Procuring that grant likely buoyed the concomitant fund-raising activities for a new campus science facility. The integrated math and science curriculum that evolved in the course of these meetings went on to acquire a national reputation, and Drury science faculty have traveled throughout the country, sharing the details at other higher education institutions. In 2002, the Mathematics and Science Division received a prestigious Heuer Award from the Council of Independent Colleges.

***

Most Drury students begin with a course called Mathematics and Literacy, which aims to upgrade their mathematical skills and prepare them for the science sequence. The two-semester Science and Inquiry classes are interdisciplinary and team-taught. They emphasize the problem-solving aspects of scientific experimentation and open-ended investigation. Course modules have included the Nature of Science, Human Genetics and DNA, and Light and its Applications. The modules are flexible and change as needed. They all involve lab work to explore and extend the ideas encountered in lectures and class discussion; for example, students in the Nature of Science module conducted experiments on "Making Ice Cream: Using the Scientific Method."

The last required GP21 class, Undergraduate Research Experience, applies the skills and knowledge acquired in the preceding courses to solve scientific problems, often of a practical kind; for example, "The Organic Chemistry of Household Products" or "Investigating the Aquatic Ecosystems of the Ozarks."

Older alumni frequently remarked to the author that GP21 was harder than the curricula in place when they attended. They are right, though difficulty was not instrumental in the decision. What drives the structure of GP21 are the integrative aims of refining student writing, speaking, analytical, and thinking skills, and preparing students to function effectively in the twenty-first-century global community.

J. Scott Lee, from the Trends in Liberal Arts Project, a national endeavor to examine causes of changes in liberal arts education, observed in a 2002 report presented to Professor Richard Schur, Drury's director of interdisciplinary studies, that the overall movement to GP21 constituted a shift from stability to massive change, and back to stability again. He contrasted this pattern with the usual one of changing general education programs gradually. His report underscored that the 1995 curriculum change raised the number of required courses 10 percent above the 1978 curriculum that it replaced. Initially, Lee noted there were some questions of faculty ownership of the interdisciplinary parts of the program because "designing an entirely new curriculum is one of the most difficult challenges a faculty can confront." It creates "winners" and "losers," based on departmental perception of how the curricular changes increase or decrease their overall roles.

It is difficult to get some departments to contribute staff to teach GP21 classes. In part this is because they believe they are shorthanded when it comes to maintaining sufficient course offerings for their majors; hence, they are hesitant to "lend out" faculty to schoolwide programs. It is also the case that GP21 classes, especially Alpha Seminar, are especially demanding, not only timewise—the seminar is a writing-intensive class—but intellectually as well, for the seminar's interdisciplinary readings require instructors to bring with them the requisite liberal arts background from their own experience, or to acquire "new expertise" on the spot. One solution, albeit not a complete one, to the staffing problem would be to expand the faculty of the Interdisciplinary Studies Center, the group that bears primary responsibility for GP21.

GP21 is best seen as a work in progress that will be modified as Drury fine-tunes it and responds to the needs of future students. If earlier patterns for post-1940 curricular change at Drury persist, then the time may not be long before GP21 gives way to its successor, for curricular change is vital to keeping places such as Drury on the cutting edge of academic innovation. Until that time arrives, GP21, to quote Lee again, "scores high marks from the vantage point of a coherent, well-thought-out, self-conscious general education effort light-years ahead of many others." His positive assessment received confirmation in a May 2004 article, "Drury University's Core Curriculum Gives Every Student a Global Perspective," which appeared in the *Association of American Colleges and Universities News*, put out by a nationally prestigious organization concerned with improving the quality, vitality, and public standing of liberal arts education.

In the 1983–2003 time frame, in all but one year the business administration major was the number one choice of Drury students, but in 2003 it yielded first place to biology, which had come in second from 1993 to 2002. However, for most of that time period, the numerical difference between majors in the two disciplines was not very large; also, from 1982 to 1992, the communication major occupied the number two spot. Psychology and architecture fought for third place from 1998 to 2003.

However, the real story of majors at Drury is the diversity of student choice. More than two out of three Drury students do not major in business, biology, or communication, and irrespective of major, nearly half the student credit hours come from GP21 distribution requirements.

## The Honors Program

In 1987, Dean Good proposed that the Educational Policy Committee undertake discussions on the feasibility of a schoolwide College Honors Program to provide challenges to those academically gifted Drury students whose needs and interests were not adequately met by existing honors work within departments. The EPC created an Honors Task Force to provide academically challenging interdisciplinary courses as enhancers to the students' major fields of concentration. Eltjen Flikkema, professor of German, was chosen to run the program, which became operational the following fall. After twenty years at the helm, Dr. Flikkema announced his retirement from the position at the end of the 2005–2006 academic year. Dr. Randy Fuller, associate professor of English, replaced him as director of the Honors Program.

Entering first-year students with a composite ACT score of 27 or higher and a high school GPA of 3.25 or higher are invited to join. Faculty can recommend students they think have the intellectual ability and academic skills to participate but whose scores are below the entry requirements; Drury students achieving a 3.5 GPA or better are also eligible to apply.

To acquire a BA with Honors, students complete a series of lower- and upper-division honors classes that parallel the general education curriculum. A partial listing of the constantly evolving and changing honors classes includes: "Understanding the Holocaust," "Gothic and Supernatural Literature," "Cultural and Literary History of Route 66," "Ecology, Feminism, and Religion," "The Human Genome Project," "The Mind-Body Problem," and "Stephen Hawking's Universe."

The culmination for program participants is a two-semester sequence, Senior Colloquium and Research. Working with a faculty mentor, honor students develop an in-depth research plan, gather a bibliography, write a thesis paper, and meet periodically with members of their faculty honors committee. In the spring or fall, students share the results of their research in a public forum consisting of faculty, students, parents and relatives, friends, and members of the public. Their projects must exhibit high standards of scholarship and illuminate a topic's historical context and social significance.

\*\*\*

Independently of the Honors Program, academic departments acknowledge the achievements and successes of their majors at the annual Student Honors Convocation, held in May, and by presenting them with gifts, small honoraria, books, and plaques in recognition of their accomplishments. The audience learns of the future plans of many of the senior honorees, what graduate school they plan to attend, or the job they will be entering. Until his retirement in 1996, Communication Professor Joe McAdoo took charge of organizing this joyful event; he was succeeded by Communication Professor Rick Maxson.

### Living Learning Communities

In 2003–2004, Drury announced an expansion of its Living Learning Communities for first-year students, with the objective of helping them to achieve their academic goals, to build a sense of community, and to develop friendships and social bonds. Participants form study groups, take classes together, plan social events such as attending movies or visiting places such as the Springfield Art Museum, and volunteer at local civic organizations. They live together in specially set-aside areas of two residence halls. Living together and sharing classes according to interest encourages academic engagement and enduring personal friendships. Living Learning courses center around the Alpha Seminar, but with some variation. For example, students participating in "The Business Scene in Europe" track learn about European culture and politics. In addition to Alpha Seminar, they enroll together in "Introduction to Business" and "Contemporary European Society." Students interested in current politics jointly take "Rhetoric and Reality in American Policy" and "Introduction to Political Science."

### Study Abroad and Elsewhere

All Drury graduates who complete GP21 qualify for the Global Studies minor on their diplomas. Consistent with Drury's global mission, approximately 40 percent of its students (the numbers continue to grow) spend time studying abroad. Under the guidance of Religion

Professor Richard Killough, Drury established its first semester-long study-abroad program in the spring of 1988 at Landsdowne College in London. Regents College soon replaced it as Drury's home in London. Student Sarah Torpey, who participated in the program in 2000, says, "I had the time of my life. I learned about cultures, I learned a lot about myself—how to solve problems and make decisions. There was a lot of hands-on learning." Other Drury full-semester programs are situated at the University of Granada in Spain, the Lüneburg University of Applied Sciences in Germany, Swinburne University of Technology in Australia, and the Denmark International Studies Program at the University of Copenhagen. In 2003, the Drury Center in Volos, Greece, opened, offering programs mostly but not exclusively for architecture students; program participants live in furnished apartments near the downtown building that houses the Drury Center. Plans are under way for semester-abroad programs in France and expanded exchange programs to countries in East Asia.

The art department has long operated a summer program in Florence, Italy, and the architecture department frequently takes students, not just architecture majors, for six weeks of study at Tsinghua University, Drury's sister school in Beijing. In 2006, negotiations were under way to formalize the collaborative relationship through annual student/faculty exchanges. Of her experience there, student Darci Thomas says, "It was great to be a minority and to experience that," and learn that despite past problems, "the people can be so hopeful and enthusiastic about visitors." Fellow traveler Tyler Barnard fondly recalls, "I will never forget the feeling of being able to walk down the street and see the market vendors not staring at you because you are a foreigner, but because they are waving to you as a friend."

Many Drury professors take students abroad for summer study on trips running from two weeks to several months. Recent sojourns include Russia, Costa Rica, India, China, Scotland, France, Mexico, and Italy. Music department ensembles traveled to Nassau and the Bahamas, and in 2003, to the beaches of Normandy where they gave a Memorial Day concert commemorating Operation Overlord, launched on June 6, 1944. Drury also has links with the American Institute for Foreign Study, which has study-abroad programs around the world. Summer 2006 saw eleven short-term study-abroad programs in full swing, from Greece to Romania and from Beijing to London, attended by fourteen faculty and eighty-four students.

***

In 1999, New York's Columbia University invited Drury students for a sixteen-week course in Biosphere 2, a 7.2-million-cubic-foot enclosure housing six of the Earth's ecosystems in miniature, including a rain forest and a savanna. At the Tucson, Arizona–based facility, students studied the environment, public policy, and astronomy in this unique setting. Drury is among only fifteen higher education institutions nationwide to have participated. Drury also is affiliated with the Washington Center and the Institute for Experiential Learning, private nonprofit organizations providing semester and summer work opportunities in the metropolitan Washington, D.C., area, and seminars in conjunction with internship experiences, often with the offices of Missouri's national politicians.

*Community Service*

Drury has a longstanding tradition of involving students in community service projects; one of the earliest, a production of Sergei Prokoviev's *Peter and the Wolf*, performed to the delight of Springfield-area schoolchildren, is now an annual event. The Global Studies minor requires that Drury students engage in community service. Their initiation begins during Orientation Week, when Alpha classes spend the day in the surrounding neighborhoods working on sprucing up the public schools, removing trash, and painting and repairing the homes of the elderly. Dr. Jeanie Allen, former director of the First-Year Experience, affirmed that Alpha classes "benefit from it and enjoy it. It reminds them that there's a whole world out there and you can't close the door on it." Early exposure to the responsibility of community service encourages most Drury students to volunteer for projects. Each semester approximately two hundred students affiliate with the Drury organization Taking a Stand for Kids, which provides them opportunities to serve at area schools, Boys and Girls Town, Big Brothers/Big Sisters of the Ozarks, and Ronald McDonald House Charities. Rick Jakeman, director of community outreach at Drury, estimates that more than one thousand students volunteered at least once in 2002.

Residents of the university housing at Summit Park pledge to spend a year working on volunteer projects. On March 4, 2004, seven members of one Summit Place team dedicated a new mural for Weaver Elementary School, identified as a Title I school, a place of low test scores and in need of community support. Both Drury and Weaver students designed the mural, which depicted the importance of setting goals and overcoming obstacles in meeting them. A ceremony was held honoring Jenelle Stocker, a Drury student who was to participate in the project but died in a car accident just before the work began. The mural shows students aspiring to be teachers, architects, veterinarians, and firefighters. Other teams designed and implemented after-school programs for sixth grade girls at Pipkin Middle School, helped the Family Violence Center obtain funds and supplies, and held Christmas gift exchanges at a local assisted-living center.

In 2001, Students in Free Enterprise (SIFE), one of sixty campus organizations, won Radio Shack's World Cup International Competition. Founded in 1975 and active on more than two thousand college campuses both in the United States and abroad, SIFE is a nonprofit organization that partners with business and higher education to provide undergraduates opportunities to teach and practice the principles of free enterprise. Under the leadership of faculty sponsors Robert Wyatt, director of the Breech School of Business Administration, and Charles Taylor, dean of the college, it won a World Cup championship in 2003 against competitors from thirty-nine nations, in a competition held in Mainz, Germany, leading to an appearance on NBC's *Today* show that October.

Drury SIFE celebrates one of its many national and international championships. Photo: Scott Indermaur

Along the way, following the team's victory in the U.S. championship, two million cereal boxes of Kellogg's Corn Pops and Frosted Flakes picturing the team members arrived in Wal-Mart stores to highlight SIFE's community service projects. They ranged from giving tax help to American senior citizens, to furnishing materials for the teachers of middle-school children around the world, to sponsoring a camp for Hispanic students. In a 2004 national competition held in Kansas City, Missouri, SIFE finished a very respectable third, but so high were the group's expectations that many of its members were disappointed. In 2005, Drury's team captured its third United States championship in four years. The team photo adorned more than 250,000 boxes of Kellogg's Corn Flakes and Eggo Waffles, to the joy of Drury munchers and the disappointment of Corn Pops and Frosted

Flakes lovers everywhere. At the World Cup finals held in Toronto, Canada, in fall 2005, the Drury SIFE team finished second in the competition. As "consolation" the team could bask in the May 23, 2006, announcement during the closing ceremonies of the SIFE USA National Exposition in Kansas City naming them the best SIFE team in the nation at helping others to succeed as entrepreneurs and at improving existing businesses. Among its lauded projects was DSIFE, Inc., the nation's only student-run business incubator.

Since 1996, education majors at Drury have participated in the Comer Project, involving Drury, Springfield Public Schools, and Yale University. This nationally recognized neighborhood school development program uses Drury's resources and expertise to improve the reading and writing skills of underperforming elementary school, junior high, and high school students, and gets these students excited about education in general. Dr. Jayne White, professor of education, was instrumental in linking Drury to the project that brings Drury education majors to Yale University's New Haven campus to hone their skills for working with at-risk students in neighborhood schools. Inside the red brick walls of Boyd Elementary School, Drury students like Kasey Breedlove worked one-on-one with students to get them excited about reading and writing. "I love the positive role I play in the lives of Boyd students, many of whom come from broken homes and live in the homeless shelter."

Jennifer Matlock Ingraham ('93) recently joined the board of directors for the Women's Foundation of Greater Kansas City. She fondly recalled her service work during her years at Drury, through the Kappa Delta Shamrock Project, which raised funds for Prevent Child Abuse America. She remembers, "Some of the greatest lessons I learned at Drury were often the result of my participation in student activities."

*The New Learners*

As noted earlier, Drury holds the distinction of being the first adult evening college (1947) in southwest Missouri to cater to the special needs of students who wished to pursue higher education while maintaining family, job, and civic responsibilities. The first director of the Adult Education Division of Drury College was Professor Wilber Bothwell, succeeded in 1951 by Adelaide Jones. In 1954, a Graduate Education Program was launched. By 1959, the Drury Evening College had extended its services to several communities including Ava, Lebanon, and Monett. The model for these satellite campuses, one that led to a permanent residence center, was Fort Leonard Wood, about eighty-five miles northeast of Springfield. The U.S. Army, which had asked Drury to locate an ongoing program there, provided encouragement and resources for its personnel to attend. In 1981, the evening college represented the largest component of Drury's Continuing Education Division (CED).

In 1983, there were one thousand "nontraditional" students, as they were classified at the time, in the evening college. Over the next twenty years the undergraduate head count for CED, renamed the College of Graduate and Continuing Studies (CGCS) in 2000, nearly doubled from 1,491 to 2,702, and the number of credit hours registered for jumped almost 300 percent; graduate school enrollment stood at 330. The figures become even more impressive given that in recent years CGCS has had to compete with the substantially lower costs of programs available at Springfield-based Ozarks Technical Community College, as well as at (Southwest) Missouri State University's adult education program. CGCS hopes to expand enrollment to 3,500 students in the evening college and 700 in graduate studies by 2010, an ambitious undertaking, especially in the short time frame proposed.

In addition to providing quality education, CGCS has been a steady moneymaker for Drury: in 1985 its gross income was $1,469,000; in 1990, $3,218,000; in 1995, $4,736,000; and in 2000, $7,889,000. Subtracting expenses results in net income figures for these five-year intervals of $587,000, $1,674,000, $2,464,000, and $4,101,000, respectively.

Varying by campus, CGCS offers associate, baccalaureate, and master's degrees. Branches exist in Springfield, the Mid-Missouri Region (Fort Leonard Wood/St. Robert Annex, Lebanon, and Rolla), Ava, Cabool, and Thayer. Two different bachelor degrees are offered—the bachelor of science (BS) and the bachelor of general studies (BGS), whose general education and credit hours requirements are identical, but differ in distribution requirements. According to Mid-Missouri Regional Director Marsha Hughes, who was in charge of the program from 1986 to 2004, "There has been an increased demand for biology-related majors, necessitating the addition of both biology and environmental BS degrees." Community needs in St. Robert, Lebanon, and Rolla have led to adding LPN (licensed practical nurse), radiological technology, respiratory therapy, and EMS (emergency medical science) programs. Since 1999, new master's degree programs in criminology, criminal justice, and communication have joined the old standbys in education and business administration.

Much of the credit for the success of the continuing education program is due to the leadership of its sixth director, Dr. Sue Rollins, who was appointed dean of Continuing Education in 1983. She recalls, "The early 1980s were a time when a lot of emphasis was placed on the adult student's return to college due to the increased focus on technology and the level of sophistication expected in the workforce." To help ease the transition for those who were returning to school, often after a long absence from the classroom to raise families, Rollins was instrumental in improving academic advising for returnees by hiring devoted counselors such as Bev Reichert and Ilga Vise. She also encouraged Dr. Gary Rader, who joined the staff in 1998, to go ahead with his plans to develop an online program for CED. Student and faculty support propelled the program from three courses in 1999 to fifty-two in 2004. In 2003, CGCS collaborated with Drake University, a member of the Associated New American Colleges, to offer joint online summer courses. Also in 2003, Dr. Rader was the recipient of the Sue Rollins Educator of the Year Award.

That Rollins was "one of their own," so to speak, having joined the day school faculty in 1976 as assistant professor of physical education, and later adding the title of women's athletics coordinator to her duties, helped to minimize conflict between the day and evening schools. She worked well with the day school departments; the chairs had the final say on who taught in the program, and some of the evening instructors were also day school faculty, teaching classes that had both evening and day students enrolled. Historically, the general source of contention between day and evening school was over the issue of quality, which some of the day school faculty suggested was inferior in the evening school. Efforts at combining the programs or eliminating the evening college—fortunately—went nowhere. Rollins's familiarity with daytime faculty and her consultative style led to an acceptable truce, as did growing awareness among faculty that CED served an important and growing constituency, and its revenues contributed to the overall financial well-being of the college. Most came around to the position that a quality education at Drury comes in different sizes and styles, while others still maintaining reservations opted for benign neglect.

Following Rollins's retirement on June 28, 2002, Dr. Joye Norris was named as her replacement. Upon assuming office on May 15, Norris praised Rollins for establishing a solid foundation for CGCS's undergraduate and graduate programs. "I plan to build on that foundation to see the programs grow and meet the expectations and needs of men and women across southern Missouri." Recently, CGCS has made progress in obtaining accreditation by the Higher Learning Commission of the North Central Association for the delivery of adult programs through the cohort model. Under this model, smaller groups of students meet at off-campus sites (or online); a pilot project at the Cabool campus allows twenty-five teachers from throughout the area to complete the entire master's in education program together, one eight-week course at a time. The first graduates tailored programs to meet the needs of teachers in the district and received their degrees in 2005. In 2004, a host of other new positions were created to provide additional infrastructure to support development for new and continuing CGCS faculty, marketing projects, and student services.

Following Joye Norris' resignation to return to teaching, and a brief stint by Dr. Ken Johnson before he was appointed vice president for administration, Dr. Parris Watts was appointed as the new dean of CGCS, effective July 1, 2006.

\*\*\*

In the fall of 1986, the Drury Academy was established to provide fellowship and lifelong learning opportunities to Drury alumni and friends of the college. Subsequently it gave way to the Institute for Mature Learners, open to all Springfield citizens over age fifty, who were designated "lifetime learners." The institute offers a full series of minicourses taught by faculty from Drury and other universities. Recent seminars include "Transition to Democracy in Russia," "Protestant Holy Men and Women," and "Absinthe: A Chemical and Artistic History." The thriving group of senior citizens has its own newsletter and e-journal and offers trips—domestic and international—to its members.

In sum, Drury offers quality education and community service opportunities to a diverse demographic of learners in a variety of locations throughout the Ozarks. The largest concentration of students and organizations can still be found on the Springfield campus.

# Chapter 5

## Student Life

*Where I Live*

More than half the Drury student body lives in university housing or fraternity houses, a number that is on the high side nationally. Officially all students must live on campus until age twenty-one, although exceptions have been made.

Smith Hall and Wallace Hall are the women's residences. Smith Hall, built in 1966 and refurbished in 2002, holds 160 women. Wallace Hall, built in 1925 and expanded in 1956, accommodates 130 women and boasts the best television lobby on campus.

The three-story Sunderland Hall, built in 1960 and redone in 1988, contained space for ninety-eight men. On June 14, 2003, bulldozers and backhoes began clearing the way to replace this forty-three-year-old facility designed by Springfield architect and Drury alumnus Richard Stahl. To compensate for the temporary loss of beds, the school leased the Jefferson Avenue apartments, which have seventy-two beds, as well as opening the Summit Park facilities. The replacement reflected a move away from the twentieth-century standard for dorms: large shared bathrooms and small bedrooms along a central hallway. Today's students expect a more homelike atmosphere, and the new residence hall reflects that desire. It is four stories tall and features suite-style rooms with four bedrooms sharing two bathrooms. Each floor houses two Living Learning Communities (LLCs), whose members are chosen based on shared interests. Each floor also includes a large meeting room that can be used for classes during the day and student meetings at night. The new $4.5 million hall opened in 2005. The building is brick and frame, and architecturally blends with the rest of the campus. Bricks cover the concrete pillars all around the building.

*Sunderland Hall*

Summit Park, Drury's new residential complex of cottage-style houses, represents a new trend in campus housing: an experimental learning environment in which student teams focus on leadership principles, while incorporating community service projects, as covered in Chapter Four.

In 1997, Drury completed the first of three phases of College Park, a $3.7 million project, coming out of a nationwide design competition sponsored by Drury in 1994 to find alternatives to traditional institutional dormitories. The last phase was completed five years later, by which time spaces were available for 268 students who had earned at least thirty credit hours. The facilities, running from Benton to Jefferson, offer four-person houses and apartments, three-person townhouses, and one-person studio apartments. Students living in College Park are not subject to Drury's restrictions on open visitation hours for members of the opposite sex, and residential assistants are not assigned there. Former Director of Student Activities Mindy Maddux said, "The college will try to find a balance between keeping students involved on campus and fostering independence." Each apartment and house has private bedrooms, living areas, and kitchens. Juniors and seniors get priority to reside there. Smal-Mart, Drury's own little grocery store, once occupied the College Park Community Center. The convenience store was operated by Students in Free Enterprise, and had a variety of snacks and groceries, printer paper, discs, and other basic items.

The Jefferson Park apartments are run similarly to those in College Park; students wishing to live there must meet the same criteria. Renters can choose to pay a lump sum for the entire year or the academic year, or pay monthly. Residents can also opt for the five-meal plan at the Commons, and wireless Internet is available. The apartments come furnished, and the rent stays the same even if students choose to do their own furnishing. Nontraditional, married, and graduate students can choose to live in Manley Hall, formerly the Marlboro Apartments, on Benton Avenue.

*Fraternities and Sororities*

In 1981, a new local fraternity on campus, Alpha Sigma Pi, applied for approval from the Drury Interfraternity Council (IFC) as a prelude to seeking a national charter. The twelve chapter members said the only requirement for joining was a high grade point average among pledges. The IFC, with the exception of Sigma Nu, turned down the request, arguing that a fifth fraternity would only increase competition in an already declining Greek system, this despite the fact that the national office had granted "colony" status to Sigma Pi. Phi Kappa Sigma, one of the four fraternities active at the time, closed its doors in 1982. Eventually, through hard work and perseverance, the Colony of Sigma Pi achieved recognition as a full-fledged fraternity from both the Drury and the national IFCs on April 17, 1982 (*Drury Mirror,* September 16, 1983).

In the fall of 1997, alumni and active members of the four men's fraternities met to address concerns about the future of the Greek system at Drury, centering on the conditions of the frat houses. The group concluded that a joint initiative between the fraternities and the administration was in order to devise a long-term housing improvement plan that would make fraternity membership more attractive. Out of these meetings came a plan for the construction of new frat houses within the College Park residential development, blending them in with the architecture of the neighborhood. Drury provided land there to the fraternities valued at $500,000. The school also agreed to fund the residential-only portions of the new structures at a maximum cost of around $27,000 per bed. Initially Sigma Nu, Lambda Chi Alpha, and Kappa Alpha elected to participate in the plan; a bit later Sigma Pi joined in. The alumni from each fraternity agreed to raise the remaining funds, ranging from $400,000 to $700,000 per house. The cost to Drury was approximately $1 million per house, in return for which the university collected the room rental revenues over the lives of the houses.

*The O'Reilly-Morris House, home of Sigma Nu, is one of four fraternity houses that face a central courtyard*

The total cost, including furnishings, for the 13,000-square-foot Lambda Chi Alpha house was about $1,650,000. The Sigma Nu house, approximately 12,350 square feet, came in at $1,635,000. It was renamed the O'Reilly-Morris House in honor of Larry O'Reilly ('68), David O'Reilly ('70), and John L. Morris ('70), all of whom generously contributed funds to the project. The Kappa Alphas' new 13,600-square-foot home was just over $1,740,000, while the costs for the new Sigma Pi digs ran about $1,400,000. The old Sigma Nu house was converted into the Donald and Ruth Martin Alumni Center, hosting the offices of Development and Alumni Relations.

The fraternities hoped these distinctive new structures would re-energize the fraternity system, increase the number of men participating in rush, and help assure a strong future for Drury's Greek men. At present, around 32 percent of the student body belongs to Greek organizations, and there are more women participating than men. That figure represents a significant drop from the halcyon days of the 1940s and 1950s when more than half the student body joined; when Karen Sweeney became dean of students in 1973, Greeks made up 60 percent of the student body. The large attrition has been gradual (for 1980, the figure was 47 percent), and though the numbers have increased, it is hard to envisage them again hitting the 60 percent mark. Likely the decrease is attributable to the more independent-minded students coming to Drury and the plethora of activities, clubs, and organizations available to meet their social, academic, and community service aspirations. For that matter the decline in fraternity memberships was a nationwide phenomenon.

The Moore administration saw its contribution to facilitating the housing of Greeks as an investment, not a subsidy. The administration hoped the "more commercial" College Park location would lead to increased coordination between the fraternities and Student Services and to their having less of an impact there, as opposed to in their previous residential neighborhood. On this subject, columnist Sarah Overstreet interviewed Bob Dixon, former president of the Midtown Association, who "probably had as good a fix as anyone on the problems that existed between Drury's Kappa Alpha fraternity members and their neighbors on North Washington Avenue." "The guys who live there really do things to try to be good neighbors," said Dixon. "There are some good guys down there, but when they get drunk, it's a different story" (*Springfield News-Leader,* September 7, 1999). KA drinking problems led Dean Karen Sweeney to promise disciplinary action if necessary, while the acting chapter advisor pledged to better monitor the behavior of its members, and the KA executive promised to investigate the neighbors' complaints and take the appropriate action. Sweeney was optimistic that the relocation of the new KA house would bring an end to these problems.

The place of fraternal organizations on campus was a subject of endless debates during the writer's tenure on campus. In response to a *Mirror* questionnaire in 1966 soliciting their views on the Greek system, faculty who responded did so negatively. Among the Greeks' liabilities, they pointed to questionable policies of the national organizations, lack of academic direction, and "worthless activities such as 'hell week'" (*Drury Story,* 332). That antipathy continues for some current faculty who regard the Greek system as anathema to liberal arts education. With slight exaggeration, they accept a vision of Greek life as portrayed in the John Belushi movie *Animal House,* where the brothers are portrayed as rowdy, hard-drinking, anti-intellectual party animals. They also view the harsh competition among rival fraternities for recruits, and the "blackball system" for rejecting members, as antidemocratic.

In the 1970s, partly because incoming freshmen were more independent, fraternities faced a significant diminution of recruits. To stop the hemorrhaging, Greeks made a number of changes; for example, banning hazing and other degrading initiation practices, and making pledge education more responsive to campus needs. Many faculty realize on a pragmatic level that the Greek system will continue to be an important part of student life, and the wisest course of action is to work with the Greeks, rather than to fulminate against them. These faculty members have worked, with minimal success, to establish a deferred rush system so that prospective pledges can get to know all the possibilities for campus involvement before prematurely undertaking a binding commitment.

Some faculty serve as sponsors for Greek organizations, working with them to encourage an appropriate balance between the members' academic success and social life. They reject stereotyped, one-sided depictions of Greek life. They point out the heavy community service involvement of the Greeks, who raise money and organize activities, often fun, for many underprivileged youngsters.

In 1993, the Greek system endorsed the Drury College Standards of Excellence, which gave awards to all chapters achieving excellence in three different areas: service and support of others, outstanding levels of scholarship, and internal programs and operations. All groups agreed to exhibit "a heightened awareness of the importance of providing and participating in nonalcoholic school functions outside the classroom." Since the agreement to honor the Standards of Excellence, community service, always a part of Greek life, has blossomed. Kappa Alpha and Sigma Nu both worked to benefit the Rainbow Network and the Boys and Girls Clubs of Springfield; Lambda Chi Alpha collected four thousand pounds of food for the Ozarks Food Harvest and donated funds to the first Relay for Life; Sigma Pi held a blood drive for the Red Cross and sponsored a Cub Scout troop. All of the frat houses held some nonalcoholic parties and pushed academic excellence on their brothers.

On the sorority side, Kappa Delta mentored youth in Springfield schools and sponsored National Women's Friendship Day. Delta Delta Delta participated in projects to benefit St. Jude's Cancer Research Hospital and made goody bags for children in the cancer ward there. Pi Beta Phi established the Andrea Newbold Fund for Children with Autism to honor the memory of a sister killed in a car crash, and worked to promote children's literacy skills. Zeta Tau Alpha raised money for the Susan G. Komen Breast Cancer Foundation and spent time with the residents of Springfield's Montclair Retirement Home.

*Independent Organizations*

Drury is also home to more than one hundred different non-Greek student organizations. Furthermore, virtually all departments sponsor clubs, usually a college chapter of a national organization such as the Ad Club and the Spanish Club, and discipline-specific honor societies such as Phi Alpha Theta (history) and Kappa Mu Epsilon (mathematics). Student government groups include the Student Government Association and the Student Union Board, which sponsor activities benefiting the social and cultural atmosphere at the school. Politically motivated aficionados can join either the College Democrats or Young Republicans, or become part of the team representing Drury at the Midwest Model United Nations.

There are several honor societies for students of different ranks, including Alpha Lambda Delta for freshmen, and Mortar Board and Omicron Delta Kappa for juniors and seniors. Drury University Ambassadors are selected to provide voluntary assistance to the Student Alumni Association and take prospective students on campus tours.

\*\*\*

Minority associations include the International Student Association, the Association of Minority Minds, and Allies (for gay and lesbian students). For the environmentally and physically conscientious, opportunities exist in the Environmental Club and Venture Crew (a coed group associated with the Boy Scouts of America), Habitat for Humanity, and the Pre-Health Club. Logos, Disciples on Campus, and the Fellowship of Christian Athletes provide spiritual comradeship. Those of a literary persuasion can work on *Bonfire,* the campus literary magazine; the *Mirror;* DUTV; or the radio station, KDRU. A rough estimate suggests a student-to-organization ratio of 15:1. Most students belong to several groups. Attending and participating in sporting events and competitions also occupies their time, as does playing in intramural leagues.

Reagan Thomas ('69), noted head and neck surgeon and former trustee, recalled pre-med students spurring each other on academically. "And yet, we all had lots of other interests: student government, the yearbook, fraternities. It would not have been possible to take part in such a broad range of activities at a large school. Drury takes you and says, bet you can do all this" (*Drury Quarterly*, September 1985). One of Dr. Thomas's interests was the courtship of Rhonda Churchill ('69). The couple married—she is now a successful lawyer—shortly after graduation.

Those students still with time on their hands can attend campus theatre productions and myriad musical performances, from full-scale concerts to jazz recitals to the sounds of the Drury Singers, not to mention the frequent Theme Year convocations. Growing in popularity is the Drury Cinema Club, founded in 2002 by then History Professor Maxim Matusevich and continued by his successor, Physics Professor Brant Hinrichs. It shows the very best of American and foreign films not readily available in Springfield. The group has sponsored trips to international film festivals in St. Louis and to the Roger Ebert film festival in Champaign, Illinois. Guest speakers share their expertise on such topics as "New Iranian Cinema" and "Study Abroad as a Cinematic Experience." According to Matusevich, "a number of Cinema Club regulars have ended up dating each other. Art stimulates love, I guess."

In addition to the already lengthy list of opportunities depicted above, students spend time in community service, as academic tutors, or just having plain nonstructured fun. Student life at Drury University presents a rich and varied smorgasbord.

## Student-Athletes

Of the seventy-eight men who have played basketball as seniors since 1980, only one failed to graduate. Student-athletes experienced a 78 percent graduation rate between 1993 and 1999. Thirty-eight of 148 student-athletes in 1999–2000 made the Dean's Honor Roll. More than 90 percent of athletes who completed their fourth year of eligibility at Drury received their diplomas. The National Collegiate Athletic Association (NCAA), of which Drury has been a Division II member since 1992 (the soccer program went Division I in 1997), averages a 49 percent graduation rate. Drury varsity athletic programs achieved the top grade point average among Heartland Conference schools for the 2003–2004 academic year (men 3.27, women 3.51), narrowly edging out Rockhurst University for the honor. Lady Panther Amanda Newton was the corecipient of the conference's Women's Student-Athlete of the Year Award. In August 2004, the Women's Association of Basketball Coaches announced that the 2003–2004 Lady Panthers earned the highest overall grade point average among *all women's teams in the nation in all athletic divisions*—NCAA, NAIA, and junior and community colleges.

At Drury, athletic endeavors are compatible with the goal set forth in the 1898 Drury charter, which described athletics as acceptable only "when used as a means of recreation and a stimulant to academic work." The assumption that athletes recruited to Drury will perform both in the classroom and on the playing field means that recruitment must be selective; that makes the winning ways of Drury's sports programs all the more remarkable. Like most faculty at Drury, I had my share of student-athletes in classes. They never received special treatment, nor can I recall a single instance in which a coach of any Drury athletic team suggested someone do so. Coaches keep tabs on players' classroom attendance and ask instructors to record in-progress grades on sheets brought to the class by the players. Student-athlete grade point averages, as mentioned above, are no different from those of the average student; indeed, they are often higher, perhaps because successful student athletes must learn to manage their time effectively.

*Amanda Newton's intensity and ability on and off the basketball court have brought numerous All-America honors*

*Women's basketball fills Weiser Gymnasium with avid fans*

In January 1999, Drury University celebrated the twentieth reunion of its 1979 NAIA national championship men's basketball team. For many fans then and now, that victory represented the high point of Drury's athletic programs. It was a time when, as Sports Information Director Dan Cashel remembers, "We were Springfield's team." Weiser Gym was filled to the rafters with raucous and adoring fans. Despite the mostly winning seasons that followed under new coaches Marvin Walker (1980–1991), who sported a record of 249–110, and Gary Stanfield (1992–2004), whose teams finished 239–131, fans longed for the return of the glory days.

One odd occurrence took place during Stanfield's tenure. In 1993, the School of the Ozarks ended its basketball rivalry with the Panthers because Drury had begun evening classes in Branson, the home turf of that college. In retaliation, the School of the Ozarks canceled athletic competitions with Drury and paid $1,000 for dropping and forfeiting a scheduled basketball game with its Springfield rival.

In the Stanfield era, there was a sense of disappointment among boosters at first, and later trustees and fans, that the Panthers either did not make the national tournaments often enough, or when they did, failed to advance sufficiently. That Lonnie Holmes (1991–1995) broke Jerry Alexander's record for most points scored by a Panther over four years, and Chris Mortellaro for a single season (2003), or that Matt Miller (1998–2002) rewrote the Drury record book for three-pointers, did not suffice to overcome growing frustration and anger. The induction into the Drury Hall of Fame of basketball graduates James Bone ('80), Nathaniel Quinn ('80), Marcus Peel ('82), A. J. White ('84), Tommy Deffebaugh ('85), Ted Young ('87), and Philip Mooberry ('95) only whetted the appetite for a return to the days of yore and, of course, that championship season.

In November 1999, local sports columnist Eric Bailey did a story on Gary Stanfield called "More Than Just a Coach" (*Springfield News-Leader,* November 26, 1999). In the piece, star player Lonnie Holmes said of Coach Stanfield, "When he recruits you, he recruits you like a son because he's taking you from your immediate family." All-American Shaun Bass added, "He was a good coach, but a better person. He was the kind of person that would go beyond the call of duty as a coach to help you grow as a person." On many Sunday evenings, Stanfield and his wife, Sandy, welcomed the entire team over to their house to hang out in the game room and eat dinner.

But since the Panthers moved from NAIA to NCAA Division II in 1994–1995, Drury hadn't qualified for postseason play until the 1999–2000 season, making some boosters, trustees, and fans antsy. Stanfield was aware of the pressure. "There are some boosters who loved this program when it was at the height of collegiate success. They rightfully would like to have that again." In the 2001 and 2002 seasons, the Panthers lost more games than they won, finishing 12–15 and 12–16 respectively. Attendance at Weiser sagged: In the fall of 2003, only 577 fans attended a Drury game with Harris-Stowe College. The pressure from the boosters for the removal of Stanfield intensified, giving rise to rumors that he would not be at the helm in 2003–2004.

In April 2003, President Moore met with the athletic committee of the board, which had unanimously called for a new basketball coach. President Moore used some of his "political capital" with the committee, earned by his twenty years of service to Drury, to get Stanfield a one-year extension contingent on improved performance and attendance, as his previous year's contract mandated. One board member resigned in a huff. Said Stanfield, "Probably had I been here only one year, they would have been yelping at my heels to run me off."

When later asked if the 2003 expectations were realistic, Stanfield, ever the diplomat, replied, "I'm very thankful for the opportunity to have challenges before me." Moore acknowledged, "This is probably as tough a decision as I had to make. We probably didn't do it well last year, but Athletic Director Bruce Harger was ill with cancer and was out and we let some things drop through the cracks. I'll take the responsibility for that."

On January 13, 2004, with the season off to a rocky 3–6 start, Coach Stanfield announced he would resign at the season's end "to allow Drury an opportunity to target a new coach immediately, so the new coach has time to recruit before April's national letter of intent day." Athletic Director Edsel Matthews, who returned to Drury following the death of Dr. Harger, said, "The falloff in attendance played a bigger role than the won-lost record. You have to keep interest at a high level." Ironically, following Stanfield's announcement of his plan to resign, the Panthers went on a winning streak, including their last thirteen games in a row. They finished with a record of 24–8, captured the Heartland Conference title, gained a number nine national ranking, and won two games in postseason NCAA-II tournament play before losing 62–59 to Northwest Missouri State University on a last-second buzzer beater. Junior guard Tyler Rogers said, "We didn't want him to go out with a losing season." On March 2, 2004, Drury named Glendale High School Coach Steve Hesser the new men's basketball coach. A week later the faculty of Drury University passed a resolution in recognition of Stanfield. It read in part, "Coach Stanfield has distinguished himself as a gentleman both on and off the court, representing Drury at its highest standard and expecting no less from his players."

Eric Bailey said that it would have been understandable for Stanfield to take some parting blasts at Drury. After all, "He just gave the school its deepest run in the NCAA-II tournament and now he's out of a job" (*Springfield News-Leader,* March 18, 2004). But, continued Bailey, that's not Stanfield's style. Stanfield's departing words were, "We'll wish the new coach, Steve Hesser, good luck in his venture. Drury is a great place to work and there are great people there." Stanfield said he would miss most his relationships with all his players, whom he believed would make their mark on the world. "They're all my kids and special young men. They'll always be that way," he commented. The former coach continues to attend Drury commencements.

Under Coach Hesser the Panthers went 21–9 in 2005–2006 and shared the Great Lakes Valley Western Division title while earning a trip to the NCAA-II regional tournament. In his two seasons at the helm, Coach Hesser's teams sport a record of 42–16.

In July 1999, Nyla Milleson resigned her position at Glendale High School in Springfield to become the first women's basketball coach in Drury history. From the beginning, the Lady Panthers' success was nothing short of phenomenal. In their first three seasons, 2000–2003, the Panthers compiled records of 20–6, 18–9, and 27–5. In 2003, they made the postseason "Sweet Sixteen." Milleson's success on the court was matched by her marketing skills, successfully using numerous clever promotions to get the community to support the new team. The 2004–2005 promotions to encourage fans included Retro Night, Beach Bum Day, Blackout Night, and Crazy Spirit TV Day, to name a few. The full capacity, screaming crowds in Weiser bore witness to her success. That Milleson's recruits were virtually all local kids brought in a loyal audience; these fans had watched the women play as high schoolers and wanted to continue to follow their careers.

The Lady Panthers reached a pinnacle when in 2004, after amassing a record of 36–1, the team played for the NCAA-II national championship before 2,700 screaming fans in the Civic Arena in St. Joseph, Missouri, and a national television audience. The ride ended when, after battling to the last second, the Lady Panthers fell to the Lady Vulcans from California University of Pennsylvania by a score of 75–72. Coach Milleson said, "Four points short of a national title. Who would have thought it? I could not have been more proud of any group of young ladies that I have ever coached." She paused to "thank Dr. Bruce Harger for giving me this opportunity." "He's a big reason we're here in the first place," said guard Sara Stratton, a view echoed by her senior teammates, who described Harger as "our biggest fan." The 2005 team finished the season with 30 wins and three losses, while capturing outright the conference championship. Over the last three seasons Milleson's teams won an amazing 95 games, while tasting defeat only seven times.

On Wednesday, January 14, 2004, the city of Springfield honored the Lady Panthers with a Recognition Day parade that began downtown at Park Central Square. Police cars, vintage fire trucks, and vintage Corvettes escorted the team with its coaching staff, cheerleaders, and band to the Drury campus by way of Central Avenue, making a circle in front of the Findlay Student Center before returning to Weiser to be greeted by an old-fashioned pep rally and a barbeque.

\*\*\*

In August 1983, following the resignation of swimming coach Jack Steck, who moved crosstown to Southwest Missouri State University, Brian Reynolds ('82), at the ripe old age of twenty-three, was named to replace him. The *News-Leader* raised the question shared by many: "Can a 23-year-old, after one year as an assistant under Steck, keep Drury near the top?" The answer has been a resounding "Yes." Under Reynolds' leadership, the men's swimming and diving teams have won eight NAIA national championships, including seven in a row between 1987 and 1994, plus four NCAA-II titles (1999, 2003, and back-to-back first-place repeats as national champions in 2005 and 2006.) Drury Junior Jakub Jiracek was named Male Swimmer of the Year following the Panthers' latest win.

On the women's side, in a program that began in 1988, there are three NAIA titles (1991–1993) and four NCAA-II titles (1996–1999). On five occasions Reynolds has been named NCAA Coach of the Year, the latest such honor coming in 2006. Post-1980 swim team Hall of Famers, the largest contingent of any Drury team, are Jim Yount ('81), Mike Lewis ('82), Dan Sullivan ('82), Sean Allison ('83), Ron Staab ('84), Michelle Langford ('86), Per Eriksson ('89), Cashel Mack ('93), Cecelia Gadd ('94), Lourette Hankansson ('94), Nida Zuhal ('97), and Chris Maender ('98).

\*\*\*

Hired as head coach of the Drury tennis teams in 1994, Moroccan-born Amine Boustani turned both programs into powerhouses, the men's on the national scene, and the women's in the Heartland Conference and regionally, before turning the women's program over to Kim Swearengin in 2000. His international background has led to recruiting players from all corners of the world, adding to the diversity of Drury's student body. Like Coach Reynolds, he is the recipient of numerous Coach of the Year awards, from both the Heartland Conference and the NCAA. His 2001–2002 men's team finished second in the nation, losing 5–4 to Brigham Young–Hawaii in the finals.

*Bruce Harger*

Athletic Director Bruce Harger came to Drury in 1988. He earned a Ph.D. in exercise physiology at Ohio State University, and had a distinguished career in the U.S. Air Force, including command positions in the North Atlantic Treaty Organization (NATO). Under his leadership, Drury added to its athletic program three women's teams—swimming and diving, soccer, and basketball—and a men's soccer team. It also moved from the NAIA to the NCAA-II. For Harger it was essential that Drury's athletic programs not lose sight of the school's academic goals. Former volleyball player Stephanie Bates ('91) concurs: "Dr. Harger takes P.E. seriously. Lots of people look down on P.E., but because he demanded respect from us, he taught me to demand respect from others." Before she graduated, Bates was nominated for NAIA Scholar-Athlete and Academic All-American honors.

When Harger and I met on campus, we often got into discussions about a history book he was in the process of reading. He knew his stuff, and I learned from him. Sometimes he was so enthusiastic about a history book—he was gung-ho about learning in general—that he wrote the author personally; I recall his engaging in an ongoing correspondence with a well-known Jefferson scholar. He put his breadth of knowledge to use when he gave an informative and thoughtful presentation at the Faculty Luncheon Lecture Series: "Perspective of a Retired Colonel Who Served in the Middle East."

In tribute to Harger, who passed away on May 13, 2003, after a yearlong battle with cancer, Drury athletic teams wore black BH bands on their uniforms. The tremendous success of the various programs in the 2003–2004 season would thrill him, says Dan Cashel. "He was a hardworking son of a gun, and this would be the culmination of all the hard work and long hours," Cashel adds. Shortly after his death Harger became the first inductee into the Heartland Conference Hall of Fame. In October 2003, the first mile of the Frisco Highland Trail was designated the "Dr. Bruce Harger Memorial Mile" by the Ozarks Greenway organization, for which he served as president in 2001.

\*\*\*

On May 4, 2004, Drury chose The Team, an Ozark-based advertising and marketing firm, to create a new athletic identity for the university. Led by Brad Oliver ('91), The Team developed a new logo to be used by every Drury intercollegiate team, as well as working on concepts for uniforms, apparel, and souvenirs incorporating the new logo. The new look retains the panther, Drury's mascot since 1896. Dr. Edsel Matthews explained, "Drury is a national power in men's and women's basketball, swimming and diving, and tennis. Drury also fields teams in soccer, golf, cross-country track, and volleyball; there are thirteen teams in all, six men's and seven women's." Drury will add men's baseball and women's softball to its list of intercollegiate sports beginning in 2007, coached by Mark Stratton and Ann Medico respectively.

\*\*\*

No discussion of the Drury sports scene would be complete without mention of Dan Cashel, the university's sports information director. He wrote virtually every news release that was sent to the press, acted as intermediary at all home games between statisticians, coaches, and the press, and was in charge of all athletic publications for the campus. His brochures for the basketball and swim teams have been recognized nationally. Coach Marvin Walker, while at Drury in the early 1980s, said Dan's brochures are but one indication of the pride he puts into all facets of his work, a sentiment echoed by the athletic director at that time, Bill Harding, who said, "We're most fortunate here at Drury to have a man of Dan's abilities, qualifications, and devotion." In May 2005, Dan finally got some relief from his extremely heavy workload when Drury hired Scott Puryear, a familiar figure on the Ozarks athletic scene as a sports columnist for the *News-Leader*, as the new sports information director. Cashel, thrilled with the new help, will continue to serve Drury as Assistant Director for Media Relations and Compliance (with NCAA regulations).

Part of Dan's story applies to many other Drury employees. Limited financial resources have often meant very heavy workloads; that Drury people perform their duties so well despite the understaffing is a testimony to their grit and dedication to the university. Proportional to its size, Drury makes do with fewer personnel than comparable schools.

***

The reputation of Drury's athletic programs is very high. The Sears Director's Cup, presented to NCAA-II member institutions based solely on how its athletic teams have fared in tournament competition, has ranked Drury in the top twenty since 2003, among the nearly three hundred institutions listed. In the NCAA-II all-sports competition, cosponsored by the United Sports Academy and *USA Today,* the Drury program went from seventy-sixth place in 1995 to thirty-first in 1999 and seventeenth in 2003, its highest-ever ranking. Drury's status came from having six nationally ranked teams: men's and women's basketball, men's and women's swimming and diving, and men's and women's tennis.

***

Interestingly, at Drury and most other institutions of higher learning, athletic prowess has little if any correlation with student recruitment. The typical student does not choose to attend the university because it has a notable swimming or volleyball program. What success on the playing field can do is to generate school and community excitement and pride, offer greater national visibility, and lead to increased revenues from donors, who may expand their generosity to include other school needs and programs. The trick for Drury is to maintain its educationally sound sense of proportion about the place of athletics in its overall mission. That means not lowering admissions standards to recruit more gifted athletes, ignoring Green Bay Packers Coach Vince Lombardi's famous advice, "Winning isn't everything, it's the only thing," and remembering that the young men and women wearing Panthers uniforms are first and foremost *student-athletes, not athletic students.*

***

On June 28, 2004, Edsel Matthews announced that Drury would be leaving the Heartland Conference, its home for five years, to join the Great Lakes Valley Conference (GLVC) effective 2005–2006, calling the move "a major step forward for Drury University."

The expanded GLVC has fourteen member institutions, seven private and seven public, including the likes of traditional Drury rivals Rockhurst and Missouri-Rolla, and perennial basketball powers Southern Indiana and Kentucky Wesleyan (men) and Northern Kentucky (women). Nine of Drury's intercollegiate sports will be immediately eligible for GLVC titles and NCAA-II championships. While the Drury swimming and diving program will continue to compete as it has since Drury joined the NCAA-II, the soccer teams will begin a two-year reclassification period and will be eligible for postseason competition no earlier than 2006–2007.

## *Student Turmoil—Drury Style*

The outlook of higher education was affected significantly by the social turmoil of the 1960s brought on by student reaction to the Vietnam War and the civil rights movement, and the perception of university complicity in supporting the former (for example, by engaging in research for the military) and indifference to the latter. As part of a broader revolt against authority, some students, always a minority, denounced the classical curriculum as antiquated and irrelevant, one that reinforced the ethnocentric values of an establishment that ignored the poor and oppressed. A 1980s study by the Carnegie Foundation observed a significant drop in general education requirements between 1967 and 1974.

The writings of Dead White Males—the cornerstone of the traditional liberal arts education—became to these young men and women the symbol for the exploitative values endorsed by academic mandarins in an unholy alliance with business, industry, and government. The election of Richard Nixon in 1968 began the reascent of what he labeled "the silent majority," meaning those Americans fed up with student unruliness and disrespect. Despite student disruption of the Democratic National Convention in Chicago (1968), and their bloody confrontation with the city police, the so-called student rebellion had peaked.

In the 1980s, colleges and universities were assaulted from within, usually by "radical" younger faculty who challenged the belief that objective knowledge defined the core of the liberal arts. They moved away from the notion of universal explanatory models of humankind's behaviors, stressing instead discourses, diversity, and multiculturalism. Their older, more staid colleagues were shocked at what they perceived to be the disavowal of a common core of knowledge shared by all educated persons, to be replaced by intellectual fragmentation: the belief that all knowledge was subjective, conditioned by the writer's sex, race, class, etc., and therefore unable to be evaluated objectively. Drury faculty and administration wrestled more and more with the dilemma of how to preserve general learning in an age of specialization, how to strike a balance between selective admissions and the right of access to higher education, and how to preserve and adjust the revered liberal arts essence of the Drury curriculum while keeping it relevant for the challenges of the twenty-first century.

Students were less engaged by these epistemological disputes, and like most Americans during the Reagan years, they concentrated on getting a good job as a part of being on the way to realizing the American Dream.

From the 1990s on, student engagement at colleges such as Drury involved less controversial, usually apolitical causes, the largest probably being the protection of Planet Earth from environmental degradation and destruction. "The Environmental Club seemed to be the most active club on campus this year" (*Sou'wester*, 1990, 150). In the summer of 1990, Drury had a Trash Day, its goal to lessen the college's use of polystyrene cups. "Several faculty and student volunteers carried trash bags with their trash in them to class for almost a week to demonstrate individual responsibility for garbage" (*Drury Lane*, Summer 1990).

### *Minority Students*

While he feels privileged to work with students here, Dr. Eltjen Flikkema believes that Drury could be more ethnically diverse, particularly by having more American minorities represented in the student body, a view shared by many of his colleagues. From the author's perspective, ethnic diversity at Drury is a work in progress. As noted in Chapter One, Drury's origins are tied to the purchase of a school building occupied by "colored citizens." As part of the deal, Drury pledged to provide a better schoolhouse elsewhere for the black community. In 1981, the *Sou'wester* staff decided to go through the school files to do a black scrapbook—the term *African-American* was not then in vogue. They found about what they had expected: There were not enough pictures in the files. "Oh, sure, we had reams of black basketball pictures because the proportion of blacks is higher there and athletic departments are better organized to preserve pictures." They also observed, "Blacks on campus do what other students do: act in plays, sing, play, study, party." In the 1980s, the African-American organization on campus—a small number of blacks pledged campus fraternities—was their chapter of the Black United Independent Colleges. It sponsored Black Heritage Week, usually in February, during which prominent blacks spoke on a variety of subjects and dances were sometimes held, to which all students were invited. The recently created (2000) Alliance of Minority Minds promotes the same sort of agenda.

Today, Drury celebrates Black History Month in the spring by bringing well-known African-American speakers to campus. Drury senior student Anton McKinney says that Black History Month is important to him because "it shows major accomplishments by black people." In February 2003, in conjunction with Black History Month, the group hosted a "Savor the Flavor Event: A Taste of Soul," featuring African-American performances, food, and festivities. For many years, in the third week of January, Drury celebrated Martin Luther King's birthday by offering faculty lectures and discussion groups and showing videos on the life and ideas of the slain civil rights leader. However, student participation in the King day activities was affected by classes still being in session, though attendance was pretty much optional. In 2003, the faculty voted to recognize the holiday by closing Drury when King's birthday fell on a date when school was in session.

That same year, Tanesha Bell became the first-ever African-American Homecoming Queen. The newly crowned Bell said that she initially experienced culture shock at the lack of diversity on campus, but that to improve things "you have to be willing to make a difference." She did so by getting involved in campus activities and pushing for increasing the number of minority students on campus. Zimbabwean student Matifazda (Mati) Hlatshwayo says a first "black anything should not be a milestone in social and cultural progress. However, having Tanesha elected Homecoming Queen by the Drury student body indicates that for them race has become secondary to character and integrity." Matifazda, who was elected Drury's student body president for 2004–2005, went on to attend medical school at the Cleveland Clinic on a full scholarship. An active member of Students in Free Enterprise, she is in the center of the photo on page 95.

The Diversity Center, under the helm of Rebecca Denton, promotes and houses programs that supplement, complement, and appreciate diversity, and encourage multicultural and intercultural conversations and activities among Springfieldians and throughout the greater community. The Center offers the Peter Hudson Ethnic Diversity Scholarship, providing an annual grant to minority students based on academics, leadership, and financial need in honor of Peter Hudson, a Choctaw Indian who graduated from Drury in 1887. In 2004, the Diversity Center sponsored a panel discussion on race closely coordinated with Alpha Seminar students' study of identity and difference. It hosted a program for over two hundred Alpha students featuring Galen, an African-American flautist from Florida, who did a seventy-five-minute interactive session that featured his playing interspersed with commentary on jazz in this country and around the world, going into depth on musicians of color. Other events on the center's agenda included the annual Festival of Friends Celebration for children who sang, danced, played basketball, did arts and crafts, and were entertained by a Middle Eastern dance troupe, Spanish singers, and the local Washington Avenue Baptist Youth Dance Troupe. It also was the site of the second Ethnic Diversity and Disciples of Christ–Related Colleges and Universities Conference.

On March 3, 2003, the Diversity Center hosted the Ethnic Life Stories Project, which celebrates cultural diversity through oral histories. The privately funded project seeks to promote ethnic appreciation and understanding by gathering the recollections of Springfield elders from diverse ethnic backgrounds, recorded by "story keepers" who spent additional hours transcribing the material. The center serves as repository for the materials.

Interestingly, the Drury administration and the Board of Trustees readily approved Allies, a gay rights group, as a campus organization covered under the school's nondiscriminatory policy statement. Its prompt action avoided the kind of controversy that surrounded other nearby campuses. It demonstrated that at Drury diversity extends beyond race, and that its mission goals apply to all of its students.

The International Student Association is active in promoting cultural interaction by sponsoring lunches and dinners featuring native foods, artifacts, culture, and entertainment. Hundreds of students and faculty have attended these cosmopolitan events, a trend that should continue as the number of international students on campus grows each year.

For as long as this writer remembers, Drury has been trying to enhance its diversity of students, faculty, administrators, and staff. Some would say more needs to and can be done, starting with devoting more financial resources to recruiting minorities. True enough—but not easy. Among the difficulties standing in the way of achieving these goals is finding ways to attract minorities to a school smack in the center of a city with a minority population of around 3 percent. Drury's competitors, especially public colleges and universities, can offer greater financial incentives and placement in a more diverse environment, and they also vigorously compete for the most highly qualified student and faculty minorities. These academically gifted groups of African-Americans are overwhelmed with solid choices of which Drury is but one. To recruit those minorities who exhibit potential but whose scores fall below Drury's requirements presents a different series of problems, from creating a tutorial system to dealing with affirmative action controversies.

While Drury continues to address these concerns for which there is no quick fix, the university's award-winning faculty remains dedicated to providing teaching excellence in the classroom and the school's renowned personalized learning experience to all of its students.

# Chapter 6

## Those Who Can Teach

As trustee John Beuerlein has pointed out, "The academic staff is a high-quality group of teachers that are the heart of Drury University. The essence of Drury is what takes place when a teacher and his/her class interact in the learning setting." The faculty at Drury, as at most institutions of higher education, often tends to be individualistic and disputatious. In part this is because their graduate training emphasizes critical thinking, argumentation, skepticism about the certainty of knowledge, and the importance of expressing one's point of view forthrightly. An old adage transposed to academe contains more than a grain of truth: "Get two faculty together, and at least three different opinions emerge."

Among the subjects of contention engaging the Drury faculty over the past twenty-five years: whether or not to unionize, the appropriateness of establishing graduate programs and "independent schools" such as architecture, what a revised curriculum should entail, what constitutes a desirable school-year calendar, and the relationship between the day and evening schools. Most of these differences of opinions, often vigorously expressed, center on the question "What is a liberal arts education or university?" In a nutshell, the notion of the university as an ivory tower whose inhabitants calmly engage in celestial discourse, in which collective wisdom always wins out and is happily accepted by all, is the stuff of which legend—not reality—is made.

On the other hand, respect and cooperation among Drury faculty is also the norm. One faculty member is ecstatic that her very best friends are her colleagues; she says they act more like adolescent buddies gossiping on the phone than stick-in-the-mud professionals. Another member describes the faculty as a group of people "interested in facilitating learning." A third states unequivocally, "We are all interested in the same goal: helping students." I personally have witnessed numerous acts of faculty kindness; for example, volunteers taking over the classes of a colleague stricken by a long-term illness or disability. This gentler side of faculty interaction is deemed "collegiality"; at Drury the word means exhibiting courtesy and respect for colleagues, underwritten by a genuine sense of caring.

Drury was singularly fortunate in having Dean Steve Good at the helm for twenty-plus years. As noted earlier, among his talents was the ability to get the faculty, most of the time, to channel their energies into common endeavors that advanced the mission of Drury. Together with John Moore, he created what can be called a "culture of inclusiveness," a far cry from the "culture of conflict" that prevailed in the decade before the two arrived at Drury. Because that culture had been the norm for better than twenty years, young faculty took it for granted, as it was the only one they knew; at best they may have heard something about the days of old, when faculty cliques fought in the trenches against each other and with the administration. Former history professor Maxim Matusevich could describe the campus as providing a "laid-back, cozy, oasis-like atmosphere," as did most of his colleagues. The words most often used by the Drury faculty when asked to describe the atmosphere on campus were *personal* and *friendly*. With Steve Good's untimely death and the retirement of John Moore, the question exists as to whether the movement away from parochialism and department insularity will maintain. The new president and dean have their tasks cut out for them.

*Bring On the Work*

Faculty members are hired because of expertise in their disciplines. In larger universities, where publishing books and articles based on specialized knowledge is a primary goal, the transition from graduate student to professor is relatively simple: Continue to publish, only more frequently and at a higher level. In academic lingo, to get ahead, big-school faculty must "publish or perish." To encourage publishing success, which correlates strongly with the academic reputation of the prestigious large university, faculty there generally teach one or two courses per semester and have graduate students to assist them, and receive a generous research budget that allows for travel to relevant libraries, repositories, and conferences to promote research. That is why renowned scholars often spend little time in the classroom, and while their names are listed in the school catalog, spaces for students in their classes are hard to come by. I recall the story of a student who attended a larger university who was convinced that professors there were dropped into the classroom by helicopter, delivered their lectures, and were quickly evacuated after completing that mission. Fortunately, it remains a bedrock principle at Drury that all faculty are committed to teaching, and their advancement depends considerably on how well they discharge their classroom responsibilities.

When I came to Drury in 1967, most faculty taught four courses per semester. When I left thirty-six years later, most faculty still taught four courses per semester. The major criterion for promotion and tenure then was excellent teaching, which constituted at least 50 percent of faculty evaluations. Other components included scholarship, community service, and committee work. Notwithstanding some revision in categories and the use of a different evaluation tool, teaching success still constitutes at least 50 percent of the current Drury faculty's performance score.

Yet other expectations for faculty have changed significantly at Drury, especially over the last decade. More importantly, the present expectation is that faculty will continue to teach full loads while simultaneously being urged to turn out significant scholarship. To put it quaintly for the twenty-first-century reader, Drury's "teachers, like housewives, never finish their jobs" *(Sou'wester,* 1980, 153). The reasons behind the greater emphasis on scholarship derive from Drury's laudable goals of accelerating its growing regional and national visibility. To accomplish them, it is argued, not without merit, that Drury has to raise academic expectations for both students and faculty. For students this means higher entering ACT scores; for faculty it entails greater engagement in scholarship, whose most easily quantifiable measurement is publication. Hence present Drury faculty members have more pressure on them: Not only must they meet high teaching expectations, but they must demonstrate greater scholarly output than did their predecessors.

Readers unfamiliar with the academic setting should understand that teaching four courses per semester does not constitute a twelve-hour workweek. One must add in the many hours spent preparing for each class, the time-consuming tasks of grading exams and papers, and other duties noted below. While an exact figure is hard to pin down, forty hours is not too far off the mark—and this for teaching only.

Faculty scholarship at Drury falls under one or more of the following categories:

1. *The Scholarship of Discovery* involves research or creative work to expand human knowledge in a particular academic discipline.
2. *The Scholarship of Teaching* entails research on effective teaching.
3. *The Scholarship of Integration* focuses on research that synthesizes knowledge across the disciplines.
4. *The Scholarship of Application* stresses research for solving utilitarian problems.

The current Drury faculty has admirably succeeded in meeting its demanding responsibilities, to which must be added the considerable time they spend serving on committees, advising students, arranging for special department and schoolwide programs, sponsoring and working with student organizations, helping with the planning of new buildings, supervising research, creating new courses to keep up with the times, and of course fulfilling their primary function of delivering teaching excellence in the classroom. A cursory look at their impressive collective résumés reveals a plethora of quality publications ranging from books to articles to papers presented at national and international conferences. It reveals recipients of National Endowment for the Arts and Fulbright grants. It indicates numerous instances of professors taking Drury students to national academic conferences to present the findings of collective and individual student research projects. It provides testimony to outstanding teaching success in the classroom. Most conspicuously, it confirms a very hardworking group of dedicated teacher-scholars and indicates why, come semester's end, the faculty experience collective exhaustion.

## Worth Shouting About

Let me highlight briefly the recent accomplishments of some Drury faculty that resulted in wider recognition for the university. My selections are subjective and constitute a very limited sampling of ongoing faculty scholarship, and in no way are meant to anoint an academic elite, but rather to convey the exciting and dynamic nature of faculty scholarship. It bears mention that much of what the faculty does in this arena involves their students who have presented papers at national meetings of the American Chemical Society and the Southeastern Psychological Association, to provide two examples.

In 1996, Don Deeds and his colleagues received a six-figure National Science Foundation (NSF) grant to revise the mathematics and science curriculum. Mathematics Professors Carol Browning and Charles Allen recently obtained $298,000 from the NSF to develop a series of calculus textbooks; the same organization approved a three-year grant of $876,000 to Barbara Wing and a team of Drury and Southwest Missouri State University biologists for a program entitled "Strengthening Science Education for Middle School Girls in Rural Southwest Missouri." Wing's colleague Wendy Anderson is a 2003 recipient of the National Association of Biology Teachers' Award for Excellence in Encouraging Equity in Science Education. Language Professors Patrick Moser and John Taylor managed a two-year $248,000 Title VI grant—matched by Drury—from the International Studies and Foreign Language Program in the U.S. Department of Education to put together a curriculum for Drury's European Studies minor. In 1998, Theatre Professor Ruth Monroe won a three-year, $48,000 grant from the 3M Corporation for STEP UP, an after-school creative writing and creative dramatics program for children from neighborhood schools with high at-risk populations. Education Professors Dan Beach and Protima Roy will use some $38,000 in NSF grants to move math and science programs at Springfield's Pipkin Middle School and Central High School to a higher level. An interdisciplinary team of professors including Don Deeds, Vickie Luttrell, Bruce Callen, Charles Allen, and Mark Wood plan to spend their $126,000 NSF award to develop a Science and Math Inventory to investigate how formal instruction changes the value students place on math and science literacy.

In 2003, Dr. Sean Terry, recently appointed director of the Missouri Geographic Alliance, announced that Drury's Belle Hall would be the organization's new headquarters. Rabindranath Roy, the Walter H. Hoffman Distinguished Research Professor, serves as a Ph.D. examiner for thirteen foreign universities and a referee for twenty national and international chemistry journals. To honor his parents, he and his wife raised more than a million dollars to found the Hem Sheela Model School in Durgapur, India. In 2006, he was the recipient—again—of a National Institutes of Health grant of more than $130,000. The year before, Drury's Behavioral Science Department procured a prestigious grant of $138,000 through the NSF's Course, Curriculum, and Laboratory Improvement Program. The funding will be used over three years to build an advanced undergraduate research experience aimed at giving students an opportunity to both do and understand science. The Lumina Foundation, through its McCabe Foundation, announced that it had awarded the Drury University College Bound! Program a $100,000 grant to work at increasing access to higher education for students who have the potential to succeed in college but may not seek to enroll. More than a hundred Central High students will link up with a comparable number of Drury mentor students to improve their access to postsecondary education.

Professor Emerita Ruth Bamberger (1973–2002) served on the national governing board of Common Cause, a public interest group, and in 1996 was a candidate for the U.S. House of Representatives from the 7th District. She lost to Roy Blunt, later the majority whip in the House; ironically, she was his supervisor when he taught in Drury's Continuing Education Division in the 1970s. The National Academic Advising Association selected Communication Professor Regina Waters as a 2002 Outstanding Advising Award Winner, one of seven nationwide. Kelly Still, associate professor of accounting, joined that elite group in 2005. Communication Professor Ron Schie was named Educator of the Year for the ninth district of the American Advertising Federation. The American Society of Composers, Authors and Publishers (ASCAP) presented Dr. Carlyle Sharpe with several awards acknowledging his body of work. His commissioned work, *Luge,* graced the Winter 2002 Olympic Festival Concerts. Charles Ess, distinguished professor of research and Fulbright scholar, is slated to become president of the Association of Internet Researchers and an Information Ethics Fellow at the Center for Information Policy Research housed at the University of Wisconsin–Milwaukee. Fulbright Professor Paul Nowak and Business Professor James Murrow aided the government of Slovenia in formulating its economic development plans. Bill Rohlf's widely used text, *Introduction to Economic Reasoning* (1989), recently entered into its sixth edition. Resa Willis's *Mark and Livy—The Love Story of Mark Twain and the Woman Who Almost Tamed Him* (1994) enjoyed brisk sales. In 2004, the Missouri Library Network Corporation elected Olin Library Director Steve Stoan president of its governing board. Sandy Asher, writer in residence from 1986 to 2003, brought to Drury a nationally recognized one-act play competition and cofounded (with Drury alumnus David Harrison) America Writes for Kids, a Drury-based Web site linked to hundreds of authors and playwrights nationwide. Robin Miller, associate professor of sociology, recently published *For the Common Good: A Critical Examination of Law and Social Control* (2005). The prestigious Oxford University Press plans to publish Randy Fuller's manuscript, *The Haunting of American Literature—Emerson and the Critical Imagination* (2006). In 2005, Dr. Sandra Weddle, associate professor of art history, was named a recipient of a summer research stipend from the National Endowment of the Humanities, while Dr. Richard Schur was selected to participate in the 2006 Fulbright German Studies Seminar. The works of artist Jacqueline Warren are featured in the corporate headquarters of Springfield real estate giant Murney and Associates, and her original paintings are used by St. John's Hospital for their ongoing building campaigns. The author was delighted to learn that a photogram of Pool Art Center Director Rebecca Miller was displayed at the Lancaster Museum of Art, located in his new Pennsylvania place of residence.

## The Little Engine That Could

When this writer thinks of a faculty member who embodied the best in us, a name that comes readily to his mind is W. Curtis (Curt) Strube. He came to Drury in 1971 and became director of the Breech School of Business in 1975. Of small stature—Strube stood around 5'6"—he had light brown hair, wore glasses, and usually was attired in a sport coat or suit with tie. His devotion to the business school over time led to his being known on campus as Mr. Breech School of Business. A *Springfield News-Leader* editorial (February 22, 1997) opined, "The man was positive, always looking for the best in a situation or in people." Longtime friend and colleague Joe McAdoo, communication professor emeritus, recalls, "He met life head-on with a big smile, confident that good things would happen." Colleague Jim Murrow reminisced, "Curt was the biggest cheerleader for other people's success. And it was a sincere thing; it wasn't rah-rah." Breech faculty member Paul Nowak adds, "If you were stuck in a hole, he was always there for you." Student Calvin Allen observed, "The reason he inspired people was because of his delivery. He can throw in those personal experiences." He and his wife, Jan, were small business owners, and founded and co-owned One Hour Photo Service, among other ventures.

Both in and out of the classroom, Strube was tireless in his efforts "to turn around this nation's economic illiteracy by speaking almost anywhere he is asked," including the Rotary Club, the Chamber of Commerce, and countless local TV and radio interviews (*Springfield News-Leader*, February 23, 1997). He also served as a consultant and advisor to many local business leaders. Springfield Realtor Carol Jones recalled, "When I wanted to talk to someone about something serious, I called Curt and we had lunch." Patti Penny, founder of Penmac Personnel Services, notes that when her company went through a growth spurt, "Strube was there to give advice."

Dr. Strube left an indelible impression on his students. Craig Loughrige, a master of business administration graduate, remembers that while he was studying to take the final exam in Strube's class, his wife went into labor. He called Strube the next day, and not only did Strube give him permission to take the exam late, but sat in the exam room grading papers until midnight "while waiting for me to finish the exam. I learned that night and in the nights and years to follow that the Drury Way was different." Eighteen years later Brian, the youngster who interrupted his dad's exam schedule, was ready to enroll at Drury; during the father-son campus visit Strube told Craig "he would personally look after Brian and advise him." A few years later, when word came to them of Curt Strube's passing, Craig observed, "Now the tears are in Brian's eyes as well as mine."

On February 21, 1997, the local paper did a story on Strube called "Silence Brings Challenge," revealing that he had gone nearly deaf from a bad reaction to a medication taken on December 20, 1996. Since then, he had worn a device that included headphones and a microphone that allowed him scant ability to hear what people were saying. Said Strube, "There's like a constant ringing in my ears. High or low voices are especially a problem. They come across as a screeching noise. The only good thing about it is only one person can talk to me at a time." He kept teaching classes at Drury, using easy-erase boards for students to write questions on, and a microphone connected to headphones for one-on-one communication. He knew he could adapt, but worried how others would adapt to him. Student Kristi Henson, then a senior, answered that question: "He actually seems more upbeat and fun in class. He does it well enough that it probably won't cause any changes for us. It's not going to be a problem." Strube also kept up his public speaking to groups such as the Rotary Club and the Chamber of Commerce.

*W. Curtis Strube*

Around this time, many of us learned that for the past three and a half years, Strube had been fighting liver cancer, maintaining privacy about his treatments, while continuing his normal teaching and speaking agenda. Bill Rohlf, who taught with Strube for twenty-five years and knew how competitive he was, described the man "as part pit bull terrier." On the tennis court, where the two of them both partnered and competed, Rohlf chuckled about Strube's serve coming "over the net like a wounded duck; nobody knew where it was going." Once he served the ball, Strube never let his guard down, never let his energy die. Rohlf recalls, "There was no quit in Curt."

Another colleague, Cliff Petty, agrees. "All who knew him considered him cheerful and upbeat. I found something more than a sunny disposition." He was a man in touch with his "inner David. He truly believed that he could whip almost any Goliath." He recalls the time when he and Strube were playing doubles against a couple of "real" tennis players. Petty switched gears from "playing to win, to trying to get one or two points in the match." While the duo was being thoroughly trounced, Strube remained convinced they could still win, and bouncing on the balls of his feet: "He would talk strategy between points." As the drubbing continued unabated, the ever-optimistic Strube kept up his patter, hoping to revive Petty's confidence by assuring his partner, "We've got them just where we want them now."

That is why he and many of his intimates expected him to pull it out in the end—somehow. For seventeen years Strube had conducted semiannual Effective Supervision Seminars for the Springfield Chamber of Commerce. In January 1997, unable to hear, he conducted his last one. Chamber official Greg Williams reported, "Dr. Strube performed a four-hour seminar to perfection." The "little engine that could," as one colleague respectfully dubbed him, was teaching classes at Drury until two weeks before his death on April 21, 1997. He was fifty-six years old.

D. Wayne Holmes

## The Man from the "Hollers"

If Curt Strube personified somewhat of an Eagle Scout approach for achieving excellence at Drury, then Wayne Holmes, who taught from 1966 until 1987, was the personification of the "rowdy bunch." Holmes enjoyed a reputation as an entertaining, demanding, and passionate teacher, always unflinchingly honest and sometimes cantankerous. Former student Robin Sprenger ('71) says of him, "The main thing I remember about him was his fascination with the novel *Moby-Dick*, and the time he canceled class for several days because he was so disappointed when we students didn't share his enthusiasm for the book, as evidenced by our not having read the assignment for class." Holmes's other literary passion was Shakespeare, especially the play *Othello*, about which he wrote a controversial interpretation that appeared in *Upstart Crow*, a well-known Shakespeare literary journal.

Growing up in Barry County, Missouri, under conditions of pronounced poverty, Holmes's upward mobility is a kind of Horatio Alger story, with the difference being that unlike the typical Alger hero, he remained true to his Ozarks roots. Before coming to Drury, Holmes taught high school English for ten years and coached football. He walked with a slight limp from his football-playing days. "Football is a stupid game, but I still love the sport." It was hard to miss Holmes on campus, where he often sported a long and bushy beard. Long gray hair flowed down the sides of his head and blended with his blue-gray plaid flannel shirt, blue jeans, and worn boots. "His wearing a suit is like a pit bull donning a sun bonnet" (Price Flanagan, "Fence Straddling: Wayne Holmes Style," *Drury Quarterly*, Winter 1989, 2). A hint of a scowl and a tint of belligerence were never far below the surface. Yet with a twinkle in his eye, Holmes could recount how he flunked high school English three times and was found guilty of "mutiny" while serving in the army.

He was a seasoned teller of stories, many of them risqué; people on both coasts have honored him for his mile-long fibs. "He measures his words carefully like a learned man, but he speaks in an accent and rhythm as contoured as Southwest Missouri's hills and hollers," shocking his audience with tall tales of farting horses and stubby 120-foot snakes (Flanagan, 3). For years at Drury, he held the "city slickers" in his English classes spellbound with his earthy and humorous stories, while instilling cultural pride in the many students he taught who came from the rural Ozarks. Holmes pointed out to them that many phrases common to the region have their roots in Middle English. The Middle-English term *you'uns*, he said, makes as much sense as *y'all*. In one story, he described the time his father bought a cow after inquiring how "good she gave." The man selling the cow assured the elder Holmes that the cow "gave right smart." A week later, Holmes heard his father tell friends at the general store, "Well, I found out how much right smart is. It's about half a cup." Always blunt but honest and proud, Holmes expressed resentment at writers and entertainers who created stereotypes about the hardworking people of the Ozarks, labeling the portrayal of hill people in Harold Bell Wright's best seller *Shepherd of the Hills*, and theatrical performances of the play, as "insidious for the caricaturing of the hill people, not only their language but their lifestyles." He expressed frustration that "we in the

Ozarks still allow and seemingly approve of those portraying us as buffoons and fools."

Holmes understood that he was fighting a losing battle against maintaining the hill people's dialect, and that the flattening of the language would continue. As for himself, he said defiantly that although a great many people, as they attempt to better themselves financially and socially, "get shed of" speech and pronunciations that mark them as having come from the Ozarks, "I'm not giving it up." A man of his word, for many years after his retirement Holmes contributed a bi-weekly column to the *Springfield News-Leader* about his boyhood adventures in Barry County.

### More Than a Teacher

Complementing the academic program is Drury's long tradition of personal academic advising for students. A key to its success hinges on the open-door policy followed by most faculty members, meaning that if the office door is open the student is welcome to pop in just to chat, to seek advice, or to talk about academics. Mike O'Brien of the communication department said his favorite place on campus was his office—many other faculty interviewees felt likewise—because "students come here often." Students feel they can approach faculty outside of the classroom because O'Brien and his colleagues convey to students that they are accessible and like it that way. Teaching at Drury goes on in and out of the classroom. Of course, regularly scheduled office hours are posted by all professors.

For a long time new students were assigned to faculty advisors based on common areas of interest, on the grounds that they planned to major in the professor's field of expertise. After the inception of the Global Perspectives 21 curriculum, Alpha Seminar instructors took responsibility for the academic advising of their freshmen groups. Alpha instructors received training for the demanding task from the Academic Advising Office, run by Dr. Jeanie Allen, who was director of the First-Year Experience and academic advising until 2004. During registration, her office passed out materials detailing first-year course selection possibilities for all entering students irrespective of major. Architecture and pre-med faculty ran special sessions for their students because of their numerous prescribed requirements.

Over the course of their stay at Drury, students change majors on average two to three times. This is because many begin college at only eighteen years of age, where a change of mind is natural. Alternately, they may discover that their knowledge and interest in the first major selected turns out to be minimal or nonexistent. Like this author in his undergraduate days, a student may take a class with an instructor who makes the subject so interesting and exciting that the student is inspired to follow in the teacher's footsteps. Psychology Professor Vickie Luttrell was thrilled at hearing from one of her students, "When I think of who I want to become, I think of you. You are an incredible role model." With genuine modesty Luttrell accepted the complement, overjoyed to learn "that I am making a difference in the lives of students," a sentiment shared by her colleagues.

In 2000, Drury began online registration. This had the advantage of convenience, and allowed the student to ascertain progress to date in meeting curriculum requirements. And, of course, it was faster than the old system, which always had waiting lines. Beginning with the spring 2004 registration, students could preplan a full year's schedule, not just a semester's. By the same token, it was now easier for advisees to avoid making appointments with advisors because the online system was self-operating. But like the self-checkout mechanisms at supermarkets, the system malfunctions occasionally or does not make obvious how to enter unusual transactions. Many faculty members worried that the new system and Drury's pride in personalized education were incompatible. They wanted to continue the tradition of meeting with students face-to-face and asking how they are doing, both in the classroom and in general. To address the problem, Dr. Allen's position was split into two full-time positions: a director of academic planning and a director of transitional planning. The former essentially replicated Allen's duties and devoted additional energies to working with College Park and Living Learning Communities, and international students. The latter involved coordinating interactions between faculty advisors and students, as well as providing students help with majors, selection of advisors, and updates on changing graduation requirements.

*Kudos*

The years 1980–2004 witnessed the retirement of the following faculty: Victor Agruso (2000), Judith Armstrong (1994), Harvey Asher (2003), Ruth Bamberger (2002), Eleanor Beck (1982), James Bynum (1992), Allen Eikner (1983), Alan Foltz (2005), James Griffin (2001), Bill Harding (1988), Ed Hill (1988), Wayne Holmes (1987), Rosemary Jackson (2005), Richard Killough (1994), James Livingston (1995), Joe McAdoo (1996), Harriet Mears (1992), Richard Mears (1992), Sam Minasian (1995), Ted Nickle (1999), Jorge Padron (1993), James Riley (1999), Steve Rutan (1994), James Smith (1991), Sam Smith (1988), Jerzy Starczewski (2002), Larry Stauffer (1995), and Sidney Vise (1999). The emeriti listed in the 2003–2004 Drury Catalog as a group taught at Drury for 666 years—but who's counting?

During those years, the Drury faculty attended memorials for the following colleagues: Robert Wilhoit (1981), Wilber Bothwell (1987),

Robert Ingersol (1991), Louise Covington (1992), Willard Graves (1992), Charles Mercer (1994), Howard Himmelreich (1997), Curt Strube (1997), Joyce Bonacker (1998), Lorene Bahn (1999), Eleanor Beck (1999), Oscar Fryer (1999), Mary Elizabeth Klingner (1999), Lora Bond (2000), Wayne Johnson (2000), Richard Mears (2001), William Berger (2002), Bruce Harger (2003), Terry Hudson (2004), and Steve Good (2004).

The faculty is not the only group responsible for the students benefiting from the totality of the Drury Experience. The staff plays a vital complementary role in realizing that common objective.

# Chapter 7

## It's More Than a Job

### *A Culture of Relationships*

The people who work at Drury make it a special place. Gale Boutwell, school registrar, has been at her job since 1972, and has seen both the good and bad times. She speaks with pride of the recent new online advising module, but also remembers the times when "the word was going around that there were going to be no paychecks." She considers Drury a place where people stick together, feel good about what is going on, and are committed to doing their part. Her favorite time is graduation, when everything falls into place for those who arrived a scant four years earlier, often as eighteen-year-olds, anxious and uncertain about what awaited them. "The culture of relationships drives this place; they somehow transcend the physical expansion, whatever else," Boutwell explains. "It's just amazing that it happens over and over and over again."

One of her fondest recollections is her role in Dr. Moore's inauguration in those days when "the money wasn't exactly flowing in." She and her staff wanted to make some gray-and-red chevron banners to commemorate the occasion and change the atmosphere of Stone Chapel. Boutwell sewed the huge banners herself and hung them over the balconies in the chapel. The banners inspired Karen Sweeney, then dean of students, to have some banners professionally made. They now adorn the chapel as symbols of the Disciples of Christ. "I really like it that Dr. Moore was really happy with his selection. And Steve Good was there, and I had the feeling that we had the perfect dean and the perfect president."

### A Flower With Many Petals

Susan Kirby, a Drury graduate and director of alumni relations since 1984, recalls the many changes among students and alumni over the last twenty years. When she first came to Drury, students could not wear jeans to class. Students living off campus were not allowed in dorms unless they were guests of the residents. Drinking on campus was strictly prohibited, and there were serious repercussions for those who violated this policy. Fewer Drury students worked then; those who did usually had jobs on campus. Today, more students than ever work, most at off-campus jobs.

Today's students, Kirby contends, are more demanding consumers, an observation confirmed by Karen Sweeney. They want their voices to be heard in decisions affecting them, and are less hesitant in expressing their opinions. Financial aid and room amenities are critical factors in their deciding whether or not to attend Drury. The College Park community and the establishment of Living Learning Communities are two of the ways Drury has addressed these concerns. Yet over the years, says Kirby, what remains unique about Drury is that students develop very close relationships with professors, not only while attending classes, but also in the years afterward. "I know a lot of alumni check in with their professors over the years and let them know what is going on," she says. "I think they perceive that professors really care about their lives and successes; that's really cool about Drury."

Kirby worries about today's students isolating themselves more in the computer world than their predecessors. Younger alumni want more of their contact from her office through the Internet: "They are used to things happening fast and they expect things to happen back fast. The older alumni are more traditional and know what *RSVP* means." In dealing with alumni ranging in age from twenty-three to ninety, Kirby operates in these two different worlds, and her office welcomes the challenge of serving both constituencies.

The Alumni Association at Drury is inclusive, open to anyone who earns thirty or more credits at Drury or has graduated from the school. An alumni council, whose twenty members rotate on and off, oversees the organization. Drury alumni Art Haseltine and Tom Lynch helped develop the structure and bylaws for the group. One of its programs developed alumni recruitment teams to help solicit students from all over the country. Members of another organization, Alumni Connections, act as mentors to current Drury students, inviting them to spend time at the members' workplaces. The Drury Ambassadors, staffed by current students, have a mission to develop the alumni leaders of the future; their international counterpart works on recruitment in other countries and serves as a contact for Drury alumni visiting and working abroad.

In the mid-1950s and 1960s, the Alumni Association moved toward holding official reunions, mostly off-campus gatherings in their homes and favorite local restaurants such as the Shady Inn and Kentwood Arms, since Drury policy prohibited alumni from consuming alcohol on campus. Distinguished Alumni Awards were presented the same day as Homecoming until a huge snowstorm in 1975 prevented one recipient from arriving and delayed the flight of another for many hours. After that, all awards and meetings were moved to the spring, when alumni returned to campus during Commencement week. New reunion activities included the Golden Circle luncheon, recognizing graduates of fifty or more years ago, and cluster reunions, which brought three class years together for their five-year reunions. In the mid-1980s, the Board of Trustees approved the use of beer and wine on campus for alumni and donor events. In 2006, reunion events shifted to the fall, so alumni could experience the campus bustle.

Some alumni recently expressed reservations about Drury changing from a college to a university, fearing the loss of its liberal arts core. Yet, says Kirby, the basic stuff is still right here: "Think of Drury as a flower with many petals. At the core of it is the heart and soul of Drury—the liberal arts community, small classes, professor-student relationships. The petals are the great opportunities offered to students by the professional programs, international education, internships, and chances to do research."

"People here care," says Darlene Dill, music department secretary and a forty-year Drury staff member. "That's what makes Drury special. I know from my own kids who attended that teachers here are concerned about students and want them to succeed." While not spelled out in job descriptions, the culture at Drury believes caring about students is integral to the work. The sign on Darlene's desk reads SECRETARY/MOM/COUNSELOR. "Sometimes I can only listen, but that helps. The faculty here expects me to listen and help students. They think it is part of my job."

Ann Nelms, who worked as a counselor in student development for the past fifteen years, described Drury as a very good place to work, where everyone knows one another. She pointed out that women are respected at Drury and hold significant administrative positions. At the same time, she worried that "Drury is a little too comfortable, a little too middle-class, a little too traditional."

All faculty knew the real source of power on the Drury campus between 1993 and 2000, the one person to go to when all other recourse failed, the only individual whose advice and clout one could count on to get the job done—efficiently and effectively. Her name is Georgia Shaffer and she truly was Drury's "master of the universe" while working as executive assistant to Jim Buchholz in Financial Services.

*Georgia Shaffer*

Ann San Paolo, administrative assistant for the communication department, has found Drury an easy place to get to know. Though Drury is full of characters of all kinds, she finds the author, formerly from the department of history and political science, to be her most unforgettable. His escapades included keeping the faculty and staff informed by e-mail of his unsuccessful three-year campaign to become the head coach of a Drury athletic team. While serving as honorary coach at a Lady Panthers basketball game, he and his wife, Sandy, led the fans to the court floor at intermission to dance the horah—setting a record for the largest number of non-Jews ever to perform this Hebrew folk dance at a college sporting event.

Among the high points of Kevin French's ten-year career at Drury, since 2001 as head of security, was meeting and later proposing to his wife, Valerie, on campus. Another, said French, took place on Burnham Circle, a hub of activity for campus life and where he wrote most of his tickets, including the one early in his career that he gave to Steve Good, dean of the college. Kevin, new to the job, mistakenly thought *Dean* was the first name of the offending party.

Whenever the author had questions about aspects of his retirement portfolio or health benefits—he was fiscally challenged—all he had to do was contact Jennifer Kirtlink at Human Resources for prompt and ready answers to alleviate his bewilderment.

### *Good Eats*

The old CX (Commons Exchange) was a hub for conversations among professors and students, where they were coddled by the cooks "who made the best malts in the world and the best biscuits and gravy, plus they just gave some down-home empathy when you went in there," says Gale Boutwell.

"Gladys Churchill always had a big smile and friendly word, would fill the Thursday ham-and-bean bowl (price, 65 cents; cornbread, 10 cents), and could be talked into stocking jalapeño peppers for those whose taste ran more to fire than salt," according to Business Professor Jim Murrow. Churchill was the assistant to Macie Blackwell, who managed the CX from 1960 until her retirement in 1985. It was Blackwell's original recipe that Karolyn Holdren, assistant vice president for financial affairs 1986–1997, described as "the most delicious chicken noodle soup that I have ever eaten." Blackwell, her husband, and her daughter were season-ticket holders and boosters for the Drury basketball games, for the men's team and later the women's. She rarely missed a game. Her daughter, Sandra Allen, recalled that she and her mom attended a basketball game three days before her mother passed away at the age of ninety-four. Blackwell loved to be around Drury students; when they came into the CX, her face would always brighten. She told her daughter that the Drury faculty was always considerate and respectful in how they treated the "CX ladies," as they were called.

*The CX Ladies, 1988: Vivian Baker, Esther Brunson, Gladys Churchill, and Jackie Claussen*

Blackwell, Churchill, and their coworkers—Esther Brunson, Jackie Claussen, Vivian Baker, Avice Krassner, Edith Coursin, Florence Reid, and Betty Allen—prepared a lunch special every day. Many students and most faculty knew the CX ladies. They, in turn, at least knew the regulars such as basketball coach Marvin Walker. "He's our chili and chocolate shake man," said Esther Brunson. Among the favorites in addition to the soup and bean dishes were biscuits and gravy, chili Frito pie, hot roast beef sandwiches with mashed potatoes, and scalloped ham and potato casserole. The ladies baked their own pies and would cool them in the window. Vivian Baker remembered the day a pie disappeared from its cooling place; the wafting odor led Drury Security to a homeless man sitting on the curb, totally oblivious in consuming his ill-gotten fare. Word about the tantalizingly good food got around and every Monday witnessed an invasion of the CX by the Central High School faculty. At the annual Thanksgiving meal the women prepared, they always ran out of food.

Florence Reid recalled, "These gals were my best buddies. Working at Drury is much better than anywhere else I worked. If you mess up nobody gets uptight. You just try not to do it again." Perhaps Churchill, who came to Drury in 1968, best sums up the feelings of all—the CX ladies and their customers: "We are like mothers to the faculty and grandmothers to the students. We cook the food like we would cook it for our own families. That's what makes Drury such a great place to be. Most folks say they feel at home here in the CX."

When Esther Brunson was getting ready to leave the job, she told Theatre Professor Ruth Monroe she had been a nurse and thought she might return to her old profession. Brunson next called an agency that dealt in refresher courses for returnees. When asked how old she was, she replied, "Eighty-two." After a brief pause, the person at the other end of the line said, "Oh, lady, why don't you just put your feet up?" One regular customer was certain that one of the CX ladies "wore no less than twenty combs in her hair at any given time. It was always intriguing."

Susan Kirby fondly recalls consuming the artery-clogging tater tots. She and other commuting students felt they had a really good place to gather on campus: "It was a place to be seen and also a place to get the best chocolate malts." Faculty, students, and staff sat and talked with one another, reminisces Barb Cowherd, assistant athletic director, "in a wonderful atmosphere of dim lights and booths with seats that had no springs." With some dexterity, patrons could usually slide in and perch, or the sheer numbers would keep folks from toppling over. The bathrooms were ancient—one had to step down into them, and the plumbing was erratic. Adding to the loving and caring atmosphere was the high-decibel noise emanating from the upstairs "women's gym." Scotti Siebert, the new head of Human Resources (2006), recalled that when physical education classes or intramural basketball games were going on, "it sounded like a herd of elephants up there. I still wonder how the ceiling in the CX did not collapse." To quote Coach Cowherd again, "The old CX might have been slow and possibly inefficient, but I would take it back in a minute," a sentiment shared by most old-timers.

One day in 1988, legendary nonagenarian Professor Emeritus Oscar Fryer entered the CX for his usual lunch. As he approached his regular spot, he turned to Karolyn Holdren, then assistant to the vice president for financial affairs, and exclaimed, "Oh, no, they've taken my booth!" In his "reserved" booth, he was always surrounded by a bevy of beauties of all ages, to the envy of his less-fortunate colleagues. Karolyn recounted the episode to her boss, Bill Wasson, who pledged to fix the problem—at Drury people do not usually have to wander through an endless bureaucratic maze to get heard. In 1989, to his great surprise, Fryer was "drawn and quartered" in the CX, bestowed with his own booth; on the upper part of the adjoining wall hung a caricature of Fryer (he liked to be addressed by his last name) by Drury graduate Kevin Richardson, with a sign below that read RESERVED FOR OSCAR FRYER.

Fryer retired in 1967, but continued to work in his classroom basement in Lay Hall until he reached age one hundred in 1996, still able to read without glasses, hear without a hearing aid, drive a car, and shake hands with a grip that made one wince. He was known on campus as Mr. Fix-It because of the gadgets he made and the things he repaired for faculty and students for a fee of seventeen cents. He also was known as the Pop Bottle Wizard, stemming from his expertise in analyzing how glass bottles break, testifying on the subject at more than two thousand trials. A visit to his office meant a grilled cheese sandwich, a dish of Jell-O, and the ever-present Coca-Cola. According to Physics Professor Don Weber, although Fryer was a nondrinker, "He sometimes laced his Cokes with a nip of gin or rum." Ilga Vise, former geography instructor, believed she was a victim, but didn't mind because Fryer was just trying to help her get through her first day of teaching at Drury. "I was so nervous," she said. "He responded, 'Come here and let me fix you a Coke. It will really settle your nerves.'" Vise gulped the beverage, which indeed calmed her nerves: "I went to class, and I mean I did not feel a thing." Drury lost Oscar Fryer on October 29, 1999, at the age of 103.

The remodeled CX (1999), located in Springfield Hall, sells sandwiches, sodas, coffee, and trendy power/health drinks. The staff consists mostly of students, some of whom prepare the food in the expanded and modernized kitchen. New tables and chairs abound, many of them elevated à la Applebee's and other hip eating places for the younger crowd. It has hardwood floors, soft overhead lighting, and two brass railings lining the countertops. Multiple TVs hang from the walls, keeping up a steady drone of voices and music. The largest section of the CX overlooks the soccer field; patrons can watch the games through the picture windows or leave their outdoor seats and come in for a quick bite or beverage.

Another major component of Springfield Hall is Carbon Copy, which opened in 1999. Because technology on a university campus in the twenty-first century requires students, faculty, and staff to communicate on a new level, Carbon Copy houses color copiers, printers, scanners, binders, and all of the other requisite accoutrements to turn out high-end documents and pictures. Its mailroom serves the U.S. Postal Service, Airborne Express, United Parcel Service, and Federal Express, as well as faculty and staff mailboxes. On the floor above it is Computer Services, whose staff keeps the school's computer systems up-to-date, fixes the inevitable glitches and viruses, and dispenses information on the latest upgrades. Computer rooms available for student use take up a large area of the computer center. Drury has expanded its wireless Internet capabilities; eventually it will be campuswide, so that its students will be able to say good-bye to Ethernet cables.

*Take Out the Papers and the Trash*

Nowhere is the "Drury Way" better demonstrated than in the operations of Facilities Services, formerly known as Physical Plant Services. Kevin Long, assistant director of Facilities Services and a seventeen-year veteran of the university, defined the Drury Way "as finding a way that works, often outside the norm, and frequently with a dash of luck." In large part it is because the maintenance crews are willing to go down into the trenches to do things not listed in their job descriptions that the Drury campus receives such high praise for its beauty from those who reside there or visit it, for its meticulously kept grounds, floral arrangements and trees, and well-maintained buildings.

Understaffed, in part because of the mammoth campus expansion in acreage and new buildings, these behind-the-scenes improvisers—who can found be working at midnight in the dead of winter to fix a broken water pipe—nevertheless perform these types of duties willingly and efficiently. In the spring of 2004 they received surprise notice that Weiser would host the Lady Panthers' basketball playoff game the next day. The crew rapidly whipped Weiser into shape so that numerous spectators attending noticed nothing unusual—just another normal game.

Despite the many advanced technological bells and whistles present in the newer buildings, some things never change. In the old days when the central boiler plant was located behind Turner Hall, the best way to tell if heat was flowing was to look out the door to see if in the end building, the Findlay Student Center, people were opening windows because of overheating. Nowadays, jests Facilities Services Director John Miller, to see if the self-regulated air-conditioning is flowing in these same buildings, the closing of windows is the giveaway clue.

As the maintenance folks readily acknowledge, things don't always proceed smoothly. Kevin Long laughingly remembers receiving an urgent phone call from the head honcho to get over to Pearsons Hall immediately to find out "what the...was going on." Long arrived to find the custodian using the upright canisters from a regular vacuum cleaner to clear leaves from the bushes. Kevin thought the custodian had been "a little too innovative."

Perhaps the most humorous goof, says John Miller, took place right after the completion of the Olin Library. The building lacked "backflow preventers" to keep water from reentering the building lines. To compensate, maintenance employed a huge water compressor that discharged hundreds of pounds of air pressure to blow water out of the lines. While the operation was under way, John remembers someone bolting from the library and screaming at the crew—for without warning, jets of water had begun shooting out of the toilet on which the aggrieved party was seated.

Facilities Services staff do not see themselves as working just for a paycheck, or to put money into someone's pocket. Red Richmond, twenty-three-year veteran and maintenance supervisor, lauded the willingness of top Drury administrators, especially former vice president for finances Jim Buchholz, not to micromanage but to let the crew decide how best to carry out their tasks. Richmond felt he "was working with, not for, Jim." Facilities Services sees their top job priority as promoting an environment conducive to student learning. In ranking their obligations to the different campus constituencies, John Miller's list read: 1) students, 2) faculty, and 3) staff. For Miller and his staff, "The students come first."

That priority occasionally leads to difficulties because a few departments, or individual faculty within them—they are the exception and shall remain nameless—demand that their needs be met instantly, bombarding the office with frantic phone calls. "They don't see the whole picture. They have tunnel vision." John, Red, and Kevin concur as an observation, not a criticism, that rarely do they and their co-workers get a call offering a simple "Thank you."

Two major projects that involved Facilities Services included the new dorm to replace Sunderland Hall and the planned expansion of the Findlay Student Center, recently jettisoned in favor of building a new center on a site to be determined. Despite the fact that technically these operations represent new construction, for which the contractor exercises primary responsibility, their upkeep, as Miller notes, "will quickly become an additional responsibility of Facilities Services."

# Chapter 8

## A Building Boom—Big is Beautiful

*"An institution is more than its bricks and mortar. An institution is made up of people."*

—John Moore

While John Moore's observation about Drury rings true, the fact is that under his presidency the building boom had been nothing short of astonishing; those who attended the Drury College of "forty acres of Christian atmosphere" and recently returned to campus had a surprise in store for them. Their "old campus" had grown, especially to the south, east, and northwest, to accommodate new facilities for communication, science, architecture, housing, and the visual arts, all on a Midtown campus now at more than eighty acres.

Robert Breech, the chair of the Board of Trustees at the time, jump-started the capital campaign in 1984 by pledging $4 million. By 1987, the school was ready to add its first new building in a decade: the Hutchens Health, Physical Education, and Recreation Facility (HPER), to the east of Weiser Gymnasium. The project also entailed the renovation of Weiser, the home of the basketball teams since 1948, where a new sound system and state-of-the-art message board were installed; a new parquet floor replaced the old hardwood one. The old chair backs gave way to brand-new red ones, while the student bleachers received a fresh coat of red paint. The Barber Fitness Center, made possible by a grant from long-term athletic boosters Sharon and Butch Barber, provided free weights and a multitude of cardiovascular machines, including treadmills and Stairmasters. By 1996, the HPER had added racquetball courts, additional soccer and volleyball lockers, and classrooms for the Exercise and Sports Science Department. In 1988, the ten-lane, twenty-five-yard Breech Pool became the new home of Drury's swim team and the Springfield Aquatics Club. Equipped with an automatic timing system and a massive scoreboard, the new facility was a far cry from the old Atha pool, the source of so much controversy during the Crawford years.

Hutchens Health, Physical Education, and Recreation (HPER) Building

Shewmaker Communication Center

In 1989, Shewmaker Communication Center opened, underwritten by a generous lead gift from Wal-Mart executive Jack Shewmaker and his wife, Melba ('62). Their daughter Shari graduated from Drury in 1984. The new building housed the Department of Communication and featured a speech communication center and a video-editing laboratory. Beginning in 2001, KDRU, DUTV, the *Mirror*, and the *Sou'wester* became its new residents.

In the late 1970s, John Simmons, chair of the art department, hoping to increase student enrollment, brought before the Drury faculty a proposal for establishing an architecture program after an Architecture Curriculum Advisory Committee expressed strong support for the endeavor. Following faculty approval in the spring of 1979, the first class, numbering twenty students, began working toward a Bachelor of Arts in Architectural Studies (BAAS). From 1979 to 1984 the program survived—barely—because of Program Coordinator Ben Webb's "personal commitment to the program and his hard work" (Jay Garrott, "A History of the Hammons School of Architecture, 1978-2004"). A visit by the National Architecture Accrediting Board (NAAB) in 1984 proved nearly disastrous, as its unfavorable conclusions on the program's facilities, curriculum, and staff led to a recommendation to close down the program.

In the spring of 1984, the Drury administration made the decision to acquire the funds needed for creating a top-notch architecture program. The hiring of Jay Garrott as the program's first director—he stayed in that position until 1993—proved critical to turning the program around. Garrott, who was teaching at Carnegie Mellon at the time, says that it was largely because of Steve Good that he agreed to come to Drury to help develop the architecture school. He recalled a presentation the dean made to a group of architecture curriculum consultants in the spring of 1985, in which he outlined his vision for the new program, "elegantly and intellectually espousing cutting-edge concepts for the blending of liberal arts and professional programs." President Moore, described by Garrott "as the driving force who has guided the institution out of the travails of the early 1980s," was instrumental in securing the support of local businessman and philanthropist John Q. Hammons, whose gifts led to the construction in 1991 of a home for the John Q. Hammons School of Architecture that replaced the program's crowded and inadequate facilities in Harwood Hall. On November 13, 2003, the Hammons School honored its benefactor by holding a reception and exhibition commemorating his career and service to Drury University.

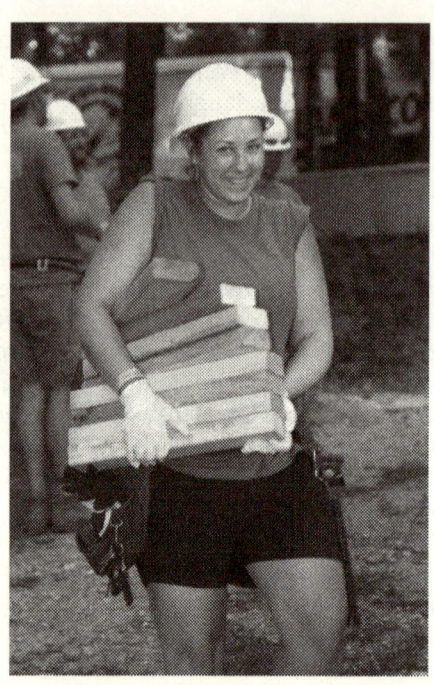

*Drury architecture students design and build outside the classroom as well; twenty helped build a new bunkhouse at Camp Barnabas in Barry County, Mo., for the ABC show* Extreme Makeover—Home Edition

The heart of the building, designed by Hammons Corporation architects Steve Minton and Jim Thomas at a cost of $3.5 million, consisted of a welcoming atrium, a student lounge ("The Fishbowl"), computers, wood and photography labs, open studios, and a small library. The 250-seat auditorium would be used for academic, professional, and public functions that would make the Hammons School an important cultural center in southwest Missouri. Graduates of this five-year program, first accredited for three years in 1991 by the NAAB, have joined firms in Chicago, St. Louis, and Kansas City, as well as overseas. In 1994 and 1999, the program, numbering 235 students, was reaccredited for five-year terms, and in 2004 for six years. Many of its students acquired hands-on experience by serving as consultants on projects such as the new science center at the University of the South in Sewanee, Tennessee, and planning for the revitalization of the city of Farmington, Missouri.

In 2002, the graduating class raised donations to pay for an outside teaching facility and gathering place on campus, located in Burnham Circle in front of Olin Library. The idea for a structure to provide for an education "outside" of the classroom came from students in the Studio Architecture class two years earlier. The Drury administration selected the design, submitted by third-year architecture major Jody Sarkodee-Adoo, for its functionality and because "it had an aesthetic quality that enhances the beauty of the campus." The design maintained the look of the wide-open quad and courtyard. Architecture students packed the dirt and sod for a series of outdoor enclosures known as berms. Students could sit or lie on the outside part of the berms while they studied or socialized; the crescent concrete benches on the inside functioned as a classroom.

Architecture students also refined their palates by participating in the School's year-end annual Bug Boil, an event created in 1987 by Bruce Moore, associate director of the Hammons School. Chef Moore spent the afternoon, come rain or shine, cooking new potatoes, corn on the cob, mushrooms, and the pièce de résistance—live crawfish flown in from Louisiana. "Students gather around him as he chops onions and stirs the contents of the simmering dishes, while critiquing his students' semester-long projects." Culinary delights prepared by local restaurants also accompany the school's annual Beaux Arts Ball, a black-tie affair that began in 1995. At the live and silent auctions patrons bid to purchase original artwork by professionals. The student-sponsored event was meant to increase awareness of art and architecture in the Springfield community. The proceeds for the galas benefited local groups such as Habitat for Humanity and the Discovery Center of Springfield, a dynamic hands-on museum for schoolchildren.

### *For Love of Knowledge*

On Friday, September 8, 1990, Lawrence J. Milas, president of the F. W. Olin Foundation, announced a $6.175 million grant to Drury College to cover the costs of building and equipping a new 64,000-square-foot library building. The college had first considered an addition to the Walker Library, built in 1959, but abandoned that approach in favor of building an entirely new facility. After three failed attempts to gain funding from the Olin Foundation, Drury's fourth proposal gained it finalist status. Milas observed, "Certainly the reams of written information we've received from Drury since 1984 must establish a record of sorts." The persistence in the project by President Moore paid off; for Drury, the fifth try was the charm.

*Olin Library inside and outside*

Special credit for the long-in-coming success also goes to Judy Martin, vice president for Development and Alumni Relations who, reflecting in 2002 on her twenty-nine years at Drury, told a *Drury Lane* reporter that the Olin grant ranked head and shoulders above any of her other accomplishments. When John Moore called her with the good news, she couldn't put into words how she felt, "not just for the money for the library, but for all that pushing, and struggling, and perseverance that finally paid off." Martin also played a vital part in completing the campaign for Trustee Science Center before stepping down to spend time with her new husband.

The new library building enabled the college to store its valuable records and archives in a halon-protected vault. The Olin Room, with a small stage, video projector, and enhanced media capability, provided an intimate place for meetings and presentations. Study places for faculty and students abounded, many equipped with computer outlets. Seminar rooms and a three-tiered classroom with a large television, VCR, and satellite connections enhanced its teaching facilities. Perhaps most important was the increased high-visibility space to display the books, journals, videos, and other materials that made up the library's holdings. Located in the center of campus, the Olin Library blended old-fashioned elegance with modern design. Red oak was visible throughout the building, the ceilings were vaulted, and the roof harbored a skylight above the stairwell. As one sophomore was overheard saying after her first trip to the new library, "Studying here will be fun." Her message must have been heard, as student use of the library doubled since the new building opened on May 8, 1992. At the dedication ceremonies for the Olin Library on October 30, 1992, Milas remarked, "Drury now joins a group of colleges and universities which we feel represent the best qualities in higher education in America."

As President Moore saw it, "We not only obtained a much-needed new library facility, but the grant from Olin also put what was in effect a 'Good Housekeeping' seal on Drury as an institution. It was widely perceived among colleges that if a school was good enough to receive an Olin grant, it was indeed a good place." Over the years, the library has continued to serve effectively. The addition of the Missouri Bibliographic Information User System linked it electronically to libraries throughout the state, making it a window through which some five million unique items can be readily accessed.

Between 1992 and 1996, renovation projects other than residence halls and Greek houses included Library Plaza, Stone Chapel, Walker Hall, and Burnham Hall. Clara Thompson and Pearsons halls were redone in 1997 and 1998, respectively. The renovations succeeded in retaining as much of each building's original structure as possible, both externally and within.

A gift by Flavius and Frances Freeman in memory of their daughter Mercedes "Dede" Freeman Smith, former director of Drury's Center for Gifted Education, made possible the construction of Freeman Hall in 1994. This building houses the chapter meeting facilities for the Greek sororities who, unlike the fraternities, do not have their own houses. The suites there included entryways, chapter meeting facilities, a kitchen, and a storage room. The Hoblit Room, named for Marian Hoblit, an alumna and benefactor of Drury, is a gracious space used for gatherings, meetings, and meals by various campus and community groups.

*Freeman Hall*

In 1999, Drury Lane was revamped to increase pedestrian safety and for aesthetic purposes. Diagonal parking was eliminated, more sidewalks and identifiable crosswalks were built, and additional landscaping adorned the west side of the lane. A double fountain to commemorate Drury's 150th anniversary, thanks to the generosity of trustee Virginia Cox-Bussey (daughter of Lester Cox, who donated funds for the first fountain) replaced the circle drive at the Findlay Student Center.

*Ghosts*

By the 1990s, it was clear that the Lay Science Center suffered from inadequate space and infrastructure for classes, laboratory work, computers, advanced equipment, storage space, and so forth. The science faculty met in the summer of 1994 to rethink its curriculum; out of those meetings came a new vision that saw science not as a domain-specific field of knowledge, but as a way of looking at things from an integrated perspective. That epistemological shift led to the decision to teach science differently. According to Chemistry Professor Mark Wood, "We want our students to be interdisciplinary in their thinking. We don't want them to think there are single disciplines with big walls between them; that's not the way the real world works." Next came the realization that merely tinkering with the curriculum was as unsatisfactory as dealing with the inadequacies of Lay Hall by spiffing up the building and tacking on an addition. As with many bold ideas, one thing led to another. As Professor Don Deeds saw it, "I don't know that it was necessarily all planned. I think it was just a confluence of things that happened to be going on at the same time." President Moore and Dean Good agreed on the need for a new facility, and the Development Office also got behind it. Thus began the quest to build what came to be called the Trustee Science Center.

The science faculty worked closely with the architects to utilize the space of the proposed new building efficiently, to set new standards for labs, and to provide lighting and spacing conducive to conversation and collaboration. The building that resulted favored glass-enclosed study rooms where students could study alone or in groups or meet with faculty members. Seminar rooms had moveable tables, arranged in a semicircle, to promote student interaction and allow professors to move through the room while students worked. Faculty office arrangements also reflected the theme of interconnectedness; biologists had physicists as neighbors, while the chemist might be next door to the geologist.

*John Beuerlein*

*Trustee Science Center*

In February 1999, Trustees Lyle Reed and John Beuerlein, both Drury graduates and the campaign cochairs, spearheaded the drive to an $8 million lead gift from the Board of Trustees. The costs for the building ultimately came to more than to $19 million, raised entirely through private donations, the largest fund-raising project of its type in southwest Missouri history. John Moore's persuasive powers and excellent relationship with the board inspired their generosity. The Science Leadership Committee, in charge of the campaign, recruited Drury science alumni as Class Challenge Leaders to solicit the support of their classmates. The Development Office procured challenge grants from the Kresge Foundation and the Mabee Foundation. Faculty, staff, and other friends of the college also chipped in. A final gift from the Edward Jones brokerage firm put the campaign over the top on March 30, 2001, just two days before the challenge grant deadline expired. High drama, indeed! Trustee Beuerlein best articulated the joy and relief of all involved in the project with these memorable words: "Yeeeeeaaaaaah! All right! Wooooooo! Yeah!" On October 25, 2002, a huge crowd gathered to dedicate the new science building, named in honor of the trustees, whose lead gift launched the campaign.

Trustee Science Center occupied 75,800 square feet, contained eighteen teaching and student laboratories, and had state-of-the-art classrooms and seminar rooms. Photographs and memorabilia on walls and in glass cases paid tribute to some of the science "legends" on campus, such as Physics Professor Oscar Fryer, Biology Professor Lora Bond, Chemistry Professor Jorge Padron, and of course, Drury's oldest resident, Toby the Skeleton, who arrived on campus in 1873 and was quickly employed by professors to teach anatomy and hygiene. Toby periodically disappeared from classrooms over the years, turning up in strange positions such as being suspended (some say because of low grades) from the steeple of Stone Chapel, or onstage performing in a play going on in Clara Thompson Hall. Wear and tear forced Toby into retirement in the early 1940s, and he then vanished, only to reappear during the move from Lay Hall in 2002. On May 5, 2004, an alarmed Barbara Wing, chair of the biology department, breathlessly reported to Moore that Toby had been missing from his showcase on the first floor of Trustee Science Center for the past two weeks. President Moore expressed his "outrage" at the disappearance. Later that morning Toby was sighted in the Trustee Center attached to the atrium skylight. Dusty footprints were visible on the wall below the ledge where he sat. He remained lodged for quite a while in his new perch, as his human keepers pondered ways to get him to descend voluntarily. Those negotiations failed, and though Toby put up a "spirited" fight, he eventually was extricated by mechanical power. To combat future escapades by Toby, after his capture Drury Security released the following memo: "Due to the recent events in the Trustee Science Center, all after-hours passes have been canceled for the Center. Students needing access must be under the direct supervision of a faculty member from Friday at 10:30 p.m. until Monday at 7:00 a.m.," presumably the time period during which Toby undertook his flights.

Toby's top rival for ghostly shenanigans resided in Clara Thompson Hall, according to those who have encountered the apparition roaming its corridors. While many student musicians who practice there late at night were skeptical about the existence of a ghostly visitor, others were absolutely certain of its presence. In one of numerous interviews *Mirror* Editor in Chief David Burton conducted in the late 1980s to confirm or disprove the existence of the nocturnal visitor, Robin Holmes Folkes proved to be an invaluable witness for the defense, having encountered the sprite on numerous occasions. One encounter took place while she was practicing on a lighted stage. The rest of the building was pitch black—when suddenly she heard a knob turn, then footsteps and rustling, "and almost a sigh as the ghost sat down." Throughout his time at Drury, Music Professor Sidney Vise, when he was supposedly the only soul in the building, often heard "sounds that cannot be explained." He suspected the creature was almost certainly none other than Dean Thomas Stanley Skinner, founder of the Drury Conservatory and dean of music from 1920 to 1950. The credibility of these witnesses—there were others—and the affirmation by the then president of the Ghost Research Society about the feasibility of a ghost in Clara Thompson Hall—led editor Burton to conclude their testimony was truthful, and that the ghost-in-residence of Clara Thompson was "alive and well." Skeptics remained, including long-term Mabee custodian John Jones, who offered a different slant: "I've never heard of there being a ghost, but we have bats in the attic."

### What's in a Picture?

The newest Drury campus addition, the Pool Art Center, was underwritten by a lead gift from Earl Pool and dedicated to his sister, alumna Mary Jane Pool ('46); their mother and father, Earl and Dorothy; and his wife, Barbara Spencer Pool. Renovated from a historic two-story warehouse and former Coca-Cola plant on North Clay Street, it opened in January 2004 and was dedicated on May 14, 2004. The 23,000-square-foot center served as the hub for art and art history students. The new entryway on the east side of the building featured a vaulted skyway outfitted for hanging art, with a passageway to the focal point of the building's 2,500-square-foot art gallery. Tom Parker, professor of art and long-term lobbyist for a new home for arts students, recalled that he "put off getting excited about it, because I learned a long time ago that great expectations can get you in trouble." Department Chair Tom Russo also remembered the long wait, and was proud of the new structure and its state-of-the-art classrooms, studios, and galleries. A student told him that "walking here is like walking through a dream. And that's how all we faculty felt," Russo stated.

Since 2003, changes in the downstairs part of the Findlay Student Center have encouraged greater student use of the lower-level facilities and space. Improvements included workstation tables equipped with Internet access and tall metal café tables with matching bar stools to give the Unwind Grind a cyber café look. The lower level is open twenty-four hours a day. A new air-conditioning system was installed in FSC in the summer of 2006, mercifully bringing to an end the endurance tests that its inhabitants underwent when the old, inefficient system regularly broke down.

### Construction Continues

Data for the period 1977–2003 from the Alumni Office showed substantial increases in unrestricted giving to the Annual Fund, highlighted by the very impressive numbers achieved by Drury's 125th anniversary celebration. The securing of restricted funds, including capital (building) pledges, planned giving gifts, and endowment gifts, was also on the rise. Some of the wide year-to-year fluctuations reflected surges for a particular project (such as the Trustee Science Center) or anniversary, followed by predictable downturns immediately thereafter. Of course, the state of the American economy was another factor. Major fund-raising campaigns have been continual, going through four phases between 1984 and the present. Phases I and II transpired between 1984 and 1991 and raised around $13.5 million, used primarily for the remodeling of the Hutchens Facility and the construction of the architecture and communication centers. Major projects for Phase III included the Olin Library, Panhellenic Hall, and residence hall construction. Phase IV, from 1999 to the present, raised revenues for the science building, the art building, and the construction of fraternity houses. When all is said and done, Judy Martin and her staff did a bang-up job, increasing total giving by all donors—trustees, alumni, corporations, foundations, bequests, memorials, athletic boosters, and other friends of the college—to all funds, amassing more than $128 million in gifts over twenty-five years, excluding pledges for future gifts.

*Table 2: Voluntary Support at Drury, 1982–2003*

| FISCAL YEAR | CONTRIBUTIONS | FISCAL YEAR | CONTRIBUTIONS |
|---|---|---|---|
| 1982–1983 | $2,376,631 | 1993–1994 | $3,789,295 |
| 1983–1984 | $1,821,554 | 1994–1995 | $4,890,557 |
| 1984–1985 | $2,798,928 | 1995–1996 | $9,571,958 |
| 1985–1986 | $5,669,748 | 1996–1997 | $7,823,431 |
| 1986–1987 | $4,808,859 | 1997–1998 | $6,434,553 |
| 1987–1988 | $3,328,861 | 1998–1999 | $7,676,943 |
| 1988–1989 | $3,606,980 | 1999–2000 | $6,455,318 |
| 1989–1990 | $3,457,157 | 2000–2001 | $6,348,548 |
| 1990–1991 | $2,439,818 | 2001–2002 | $6,504,164 |
| 1991–1992 | $10,609,305 | 2002–2003 | $13,474,558 |
| 1992–1993 | $7,548,609 | | |

On June 9, 2004, bulldozers and backhoes began clearing the way for more modern student housing, as demolition began on Sunderland Hall. The new $4.5 million residence opened in 2005. As mentioned in Chapter Five, this building differed vastly from the dormitories of old.

The Parsonage (for the Congregational Church), a Late Victorian home built in 1907 and located across from the President's House and College Park, was converted into a bed-and-breakfast facility for the university in the mid-1990s. Its lovingly renovated guest rooms were furnished with period antiques, as were the two parlors and downstairs dining room. The completely modernized kitchen allowed catering for the special events periodically held at the home.

In all of its building projects, Drury went to special lengths to retain not only the architectural integrity of the campus, but the spaces between the buildings. The grounds were meticulously maintained. Drury recently renewed its American Tree Farm Certification recognizing its substantial variety of oak, hickory, maple, and walnut trees, intermixed with persimmon, catalpa, elm, and other species. The university remained committed to preserving its treasure trove of trees and flowers as it contemplated renovation projects and the construction of new facilities.

The major construction projects undertaken by the university over the past two decades had an appreciable economic impact on the Springfield community. Add to that an operating budget of around $40 million (as of fall 2003), an annual payroll of some $16.2 million, 1,500-plus day students and 3,000 evening students who brought their dollars to the home campus and satellite branches at Fort Leonard Wood, Rolla, Lebanon, Thayer, Aurora, and Stockton, and it became clear that Drury substantially contributed to the economic development of the Greater Ozarks.

Drury's Master Plan for future construction projects and renovations was divided into three phases spanning a ten-year period. It called for a new student center, and pedestrian walkways across Benton for students coming to campus from apartments and fraternity houses. It envisioned a new business school at the corner of Central Avenue across from Shewmaker Communication Center, a theatre to replace the current facility in Breech, and a greenway on the east end of campus connecting it to Jordan Valley park.

On July 11, 2005, Drury announced that ADM Alliance Nutrition would donate 8.1 acres of land and its Tindle Mills facility to the university. Drury planned to use a portion of the land for the Ozark Greenways trail to connect Silver Spring Park and Jordan Valley Park, with public parking made available for those using the trail. The gift provided yet another opportunity for Drury to support the ongoing development of central Springfield. Discussions quickly got under way on campus as to how Drury would use the remaining acreage. New Drury President John Sellars said, "We look forward to the day this expansion will extend south to Jordan Valley Park and the downtown. We also appreciate the opportunity to expand the Drury campus in ways that will benefit the larger community."

# Chapter 9

## Into the Twenty-First Century

In 2004, President Moore announced that he planned to retire at the end of the 2005–2006 academic year, a decision subsequently amended to his departing by the end of the 2004–2005 academic year. Drury University announced the creation of a presidential search committee in late October 2004, which consisted of eight trustees, three faculty, one administrator, and one student. Trustee John Beuerlein, the chair of the search committee, reported on December 15, 2004, that the committee had selected the consulting firm Issacson, Miller to assist in finding the next president of Drury University. Issacson, Miller had worked with a number of excellent liberal arts schools—Colorado College, Gettysburg College, Connecticut College, and Reed College, among others—in their presidential searches. Plans called for evaluating and interviewing the candidates in the spring of 2005 and having a new president at the helm by the time school opened in the fall of 2005. In May 2005, the Board of Trustees unanimously voted to appoint John D. Sellars as the fifteenth president of Drury. Sellars, a Missouri native and scholar of successful small colleges, was the vice president for institutional advancement at Syracuse University. He assumed his new duties the following month.

*John D. Sellars, the fifteenth president of Drury*

As we saw, especially in Chapter Two, selecting the right president for Drury is by no means an easy task. President Moore and his two predecessors assumed their offices at a time when Drury College was experiencing profound financial and morale problems. The tenures of presidents Bartholomy and Crawford ended in controversy and left Drury's future problematic. President Moore's replacement would inherit a university that in many ways reached its apogee in the long history of Drury College: solid financial resources, growing student enrollment, strengthened and expanded academic programs, a first-rate faculty, and an ongoing building boom. The new president's tasks would be to sustain, if not accelerate, these impressive achievements.

The organization and succession plan, effective as of January 1, 2004, also called for establishing the new position of provost (held by Dr. Stephen Good until his death in February 2004), under whom would serve the associate dean of the college, Charles Taylor. Former dean of students Karen Sweeney became executive assistant to President Moore to help him with operational details while he was to spend more time on development issues and fund-raising. In late October 2004, visits to campus by two candidates for the provost position failed to achieve clear consensus among faculty that either was the right person for the job. President Moore announced that he had decided to call off the provost search; it was never opened again. He announced that Charles Taylor would continue to serve as dean of the college and as acting vice president for academic affairs. Dean Taylor, in turn, opened a search for a new associate dean of the college, which was filled by the appointment of Professor of Physics Bruce Callen late in the fall of 2004. In February 2006, following an international search, President Sellars concluded that Taylor, acting vice president and dean of the college, was the best man for the job and announced his permanent appointment.

*Karen Sweeney*

*Krystal Compas*

*Paul Carney*

With the retirement of Karen Sweeney in April 2006, after thirty-three years of service to Drury, the new Drury president announced that Dr. Krystal Compas would move from her position as vice president for enrollment management to assistant to the president as of June 1. Paul Carney took her place. Compas's new job involved helping to build and strengthen relationships with donors and alumni, and participating in "a strategic planning process that will set Drury's course over the next five to ten years."

*Needs Versus Resources*

During Moore's tenure, the university endowment grew substantially and contributed significantly to the financial health of the school, as Table 3 shows below. In his first year, 1983–1984, the endowment stood at roughly $11 million. By 1987–1988, it leaped to $25 million. Five years later, it had doubled to nearly $49 million. By 1999–2000, it totaled more than $95 million, hitting an all-time high of $102 million in the quarter ending on December 31, 1999. A declining stock market contributed to push the number down to around $75 million as of 2003, not fluctuating much since then. From 1990 to 2002, Drury drew from the endowment 6 percent of a three-year moving average to use for annual operating expenses. From 2000 through 2004, the school decreased the draw by .25 percent annually to get to a target rate of 5 percent by the 2005–2006 academic year. These measures aimed to protect the value of the endowment corpus, and reflected the school's improved finances over the last fifteen years.

While most educators would agree with Moore that the endowment "is the keel that maintains the steady ship," bear in mind that every million dollars raised provides only $50,000 to the annual fund that supports school programs, roughly the equivalent of a single entry-level faculty position including salary and benefits. Barring the acquisition of a stupendous endowment gift (or series of gifts) that would suddenly raise the current endowment to a desired figure of between $250 and 300 million, an unlikely occurrence, the present slow but steady increase in the endowment will not eliminate the tensions between the financial needs of the college and its financial resources. More feasible, according to many board members, though by no means easy, would have been a goal of an endowment of between $175 and $200 million before Moore retired. That objective was not achieved. Under the Sellars administration, Pete Radecki (the new vice president of institutional advancement) and his team began preparations for a new comprehensive fund-raising campaign. He and his team reviewed, prioritized, and turned over to Drury's development professionals a list of eight hundred prospects. Invitees from the list would participate in a series of presidential roundtable discussions, providing input in making a case for and coming up with a tactical plan for the campaign.

*Table 3: Endowment Portfolio History, 1982–2005\**

| YEAR | VALUE | YEAR | VALUE |
|---|---|---|---|
| 1982–1983 | $10,978,000 | 1994–1995 | $66,554,000 |
| 1983–1984 | $11,537,000 | 1995–1996 | $79,737,000 |
| 1984–1985 | $14,551,000 | 1996–1997 | $91,545,000 |
| 1985–1986 | $21,694,000 | 1997–1998 | $93,183,000 |
| 1986–1987 | $20,879,000 | 1998–1999 | $85,225,000 |
| 1987–1988 | $24,879,000 | 1999–2000 | $95,171,000 |
| 1988–1989 | $26,605,000 | 2000–2001 | $87,745,000 |
| 1989–1990 | $30,906,000 | 2001–2002 | $69,259,000 |
| 1990–1991 | $38,180,000 | 2002–2003 | $74,548,000 |
| 1991–1992 | $45,046,000 | 2003–2004 | $76,908,000 |
| 1992–1993 | $48,891,000 | 2004–2005 | $74,908,000 |
| 1993–1994 | $55,965,000 | | |

\*The value of Drury's portfolio, for the most part, parallels the rise and fall of prices on the New York Stock Exchange. The earlier figures include investment monies, which since 2000 are no longer counted as part of the endowment total.

The percentages of giving by alumni to the undergraduate programs from 1981 to 2002 ran from a low of 18 percent in 1981 to more than 40 percent from 1994 to 1997. More recently, the figure hovered around 30 percent. Though a variety of factors account for the variations, nevertheless alumni giving (as of January 2004 Drury had graduated 19,240 students) both in the numbers contributing and the amounts collected appeared to be on the low side, especially when matched against the figures for institutions Drury aspired to emulate. Clearly this was an area that called for significant improvement, not only for the additional revenues, but because the percentage of giving critically affects Drury's success in obtaining grants from corporations and other external donors.

Table 4: Percentages of Alumni Support, 1981–2003*

| YEAR | PERCENTAGE | YEAR | PERCENTAGE |
|---|---|---|---|
| 1981–1982 | 18 | 1992–1993 | 37 |
| 1982–1983 | 23 | 1993–1994 | 39 |
| 1983–1984 | 23 | 1994–1995 | 44 |
| 1984–1985 | 24 | 1995–1996 | 40 |
| 1985–1986 | 25 | 1996–1997 | 40 |
| 1986–1987 | 29 | 1997–1998 | 34 |
| 1987–1988 | 29 | 1998–1999 | 32 |
| 1988–1989 | 32 | 1999–2000 | 34 |
| 1989–1990 | 33 | 2000–2001 | 32 |
| 1990–1991 | 33 | 2001–2002 | 31 |
| 1991–1992 | 35 | 2002–2003 | 25 |

*Based on the number of people solicited. Prior to 2002–2003, the percentage of alumni giving was based on the number of day school alumni solicited.

In essence, Drury remains a tuition-driven institution. Anywhere from 66 to 80 percent of Drury's budget comes from student fees, depending on whether the calculations include monies recycled as institutional aid. In the Moore years from 1983 to 2003, tuition went from $3,875 to $12,995, an increase of $9,120 over two decades, an average per annum rate hike of about $450, or 235 percent for the entire period. During the same twenty-year period, the Consumer Price Index rose from 100.2 to 183.5, an increase of approximately 83 percent. Subtracting the CPI percentage increase from the cumulative tuition percentage increase means that over a twenty-year period tuition has gone up 152 percent, or roughly 7.1 percent per annum. Because Drury students receive financial aid from both the university and state and federal governments, they, of course, do not wind up bearing all of the increased tuition costs.

Despite the steadily rising tuition, the number of students attending the day school grew from 954 at the beginning of Moore's tenure to a record figure of 1,584 in his final year. When the 3,006 students enrolled in the Continuing Studies programs were added in, the total number of students enrolled on Drury campuses in 2005 reached an all-time high of 4,900. As Table 1 (see Chapter Three) shows, the surge in new student enrollments took off in 1987, in the fifth year of Moore's presidency. Enrollment increased in sixteen of the last twenty years between 1987 and 2006. Certainly that is good news tempered by the fact that while growth in enrollment numbers was steady, it also tended to be relatively slow.

Moreover, the market for students remains more competitive than ever; hence Drury needs to give out more financial aid to hold its own with its competitors (public institutions such as Truman State University and so-called second-tier liberal arts colleges such as Cornell College, Hendrix, and Illinois Wesleyan, not to mention independent regional universities that include Drake, Creighton, and the University of Tulsa). According to a Drury recruiter, "Earlier we recruited the kids, now we market the school"—which raises the costs for bringing students to campus. To enhance its search for students, the Office of Admission has expanded its geographic base. Besides sending school representatives to area towns and Springfield schools, recruiters are now active in virtually every state. Dr. Krystal Compas put a strategic plan in place to enhance enrollments. It called for integrating several staff organizations to assure that they worked toward fostering a climate where every student was of primary importance, from admissions, to financial aid, to marketing, to student services, to alumni development, to academic affairs. In 2003, a marketing coordinator was hired to work in the area of University Communications. Dr. Carney looked at new strategies for scholarships tied to widening Drury's recruitment base.

As anyone working in admissions will readily acknowledge, it is much more cost-effective to retain students than to recruit new ones. Between 1983 and 1986, Drury's five-year graduation rate for students who began school in any of those years was around 50 percent. As Table 5 below shows, the numbers rose to 55 percent in 1987 and 63 percent in 1992, reaching a record 64 percent in 1997. In 1985, Drury began tracking its six-year graduation rates, which grew from 51 percent then to 67 percent by 1992, holding at 65 percent in 2002.

*Table 5: Graduation Rates, 1983–2002*

| YEAR | FIVE-YEAR | SIX-YEAR | YEAR | FIVE-YEAR | SIX-YEAR |
|---|---|---|---|---|---|
| 1983 | 52 | N/A | 1993 | 59 | 61 |
| 1984 | 50 | N/A | 1994 | 56 | 58 |
| 1985 | 49 | 51 | 1995 | 60 | 63 |
| 1986 | 50 | 51 | 1996 | 63 | 65 |
| 1987 | 55 | N/A | 1997 | 64 | 65 |
| 1988 | 53 | 53 | 1998 | 64 | 61 |
| 1989 | 57 | N/A | 1999 | 62.5 | 62 |
| 1990 | 57 | N/A | 2000 | N/A | 63 |
| 1991 | 53 | 57 | 2001 | N/A | 65 |
| 1992 | 63 | 67 | 2002 | N/A | 65 |

Table 6 shows second-year retention rates for first-year students, which jumped from a low of 69 percent in 1986 to 81 percent the next year.

*Table 6: Second-Year Retention Rates, 1983–2004\**

| YEAR | RATE | YEAR | RATE |
|---|---|---|---|
| 1983 | 72 | 1994 | 80 |
| 1984 | 75 | 1995 | 81 |
| 1985 | 74 | 1996 | 79 |
| 1986 | 69 | 1997 | 81 |
| 1987 | 81 | 1998 | 81 |
| 1988 | 71 | 1999 | 80 |
| 1989 | 77 | 2000 | 81 |
| 1990 | 76 | 2001 | 83 |
| 1991 | 74 | 2002 | 83 |
| 1992 | 81 | 2003 | 81 |
| 1993 | 81 | 2004 | 78 |

*\*Each year refers to the corresponding freshman class.*

Increasing student retention rates substantially will be hard to achieve. Students withdraw from college early for myriad reasons. They may dislike the place, experience family problems or the breakup of a relationship, change majors, or want time to "find" themselves. It is impossible to point to any single factor that, if remedied, would lead to dramatic turnarounds in students staying put at

Drury. In other words, the school can do all the right things professionals recommend for retaining students, and not appear to be making dramatic progress. Some experts have suggested that retention most directly correlates with the difficulty of getting into a particular college or university. The more students invest of themselves obtaining a place at their school of choice, the more likely they are not to leave after being admitted. Certainly Drury has become more selective in recent years, as measured by the ACT scores and high school records of its entering classes. But it was not yet in the same league as the Amhersts, Williamses, Macalesters, and Grinnells. As former trustee Chuck Wells perceptively noted, "As a non-Springfieldian, I have always felt that the school's greatest strength and greatest weakness is the focus on being a Springfield institution." Fellow trustee Dr. Loren Broaddus, while proud of Drury's growing strengths, concurred, "We remain a regional school." Therein lies the dilemma: The more non-regional Drury becomes, the greater the probable retention rate; at the same time, the more "national" it grows, the higher the risk of alienating the special relationship Drury enjoys from its connections with Springfield and the surrounding communities. Another board member observed that Drury's current situation was quite strong from the standpoint of its "value proportion to its students, its facilities, and its finances, but the biggest challenge would be to parlay that 'value proportion' to future students so that Drury had a national perspective and not just a regional one." The unraveling of this Gordian knot lies in following both tracks simultaneously, and moving back and forth between them as contingency and exigency warrant.

The question lingers: How often and by how much can tuition be raised? At first glance, the easiest way to augment considerably the financial picture of a tuition-driven school such as Drury is to raise student costs to the levels at comparable schools. Among the Best Buy schools listed by *U.S. News and World Report* in its category, Drury's tuition is lower by one-third to one-half. That strategy comes with risks, however, given the market conditions in the area Drury primarily serves—Drury obviously doesn't wish to price itself out of the market.

Another possibility is to increase the number of students attending Drury. According to Jim Buchholz in 2000, Drury—given its resources—could most efficiently accommodate 1,800 students without sacrificing its emphasis on personalized education and the feelings of community that develop from the 15:1 student-faculty ratio. Doing that, of course, would require the hiring of additional faculty and staff, but not so many as to deplete the added revenues.

During its first fifty to seventy-five years, the college as often as not lived hand-to-mouth financially. Today, Drury still faces a budget challenge of a different sort. Continuing to grow and develop while maintaining a reputation for excellence requires the institution to expand its resources and improve its programs. The more prestigious Drury becomes, the greater the pressure to match the rising expectations of its clientele and the public. As President Moore put it, "Expectations always seem to climb at the same rate or faster than what you are doing." More financial resources become necessary to simply stay in place, let alone to move ahead.

*Drury's Strategic Plan*

The Drury Strategic Plan, unveiled in 2000, aspired to solidify the gains achieved over the past decade and to shape Drury's future consistent with its values and heritage, while moving the school toward providing even higher-quality education. Two years in the making, and a part of the preparation for the ten-year accreditation visit of the North Central Association, the process involved all of the constituents of the university—administration, students, faculty, staff, board members, and alumni. Subject to annual review, the plan sought to identify the achievements of the college and focus attention on detailed planning for future years. It indicated awareness that Drury had to be responsive to the changing education environment.

The plan reaffirmed the school's mission statement approved by the faculty and board on April 18, 1989. It called for the establishment of the Center for Faculty Excellence, with the purposes of sharing cutting-edge pedagogy with faculty and aiding in the writing of grant proposals. Its first director was Peggy Catron-Ping; she resigned her position in 2000 and was not replaced. The plan advocated greater interdisciplinary activity among faculty, both in teaching and publication. It reaffirmed the importance of faculty scholarship, and raised the question of whether increased publishing demands placed on faculty necessitated a reduction in course loads.

To raise the level of student culture, the plan proposed raising academic standards, using the Honors Program classes as a model. It urged that more attention be paid to improving student writing skills and strengthening the connections of the senior seminar experience to Global Perspective classes. It urged that student mentor programs be enhanced, especially those in which upper-class students tutored younger ones.

To showcase Drury to its constituencies—present and future—the plan emphasized increasing the public visibility of Drury faculty while showcasing its distinctive programs, so-called peaks of excellence—such as architecture and science, and the Comer Project. Raising alumni cognizance of the new curriculum and its global dimensions—and how it differed from theirs—also received priority, as did the effort to convey the "specialness" of the school, such as the low faculty-student ratio and the internships and independent projects students worked on with their professors.

The plan also set forth a working list of possible new programs. Those already put in place included new majors in computer systems and computer information science, along with music therapy. Expanding opportunities for study abroad resulted in increased foreign-language opportunities consistent with the new curriculum's emphasis on inculcating students with a global perspective. Master's programs in communication and criminology joined those already existing in business and education. Remaining on the drawing board were future degree-granting programs in the fields of allied health.

The plan established quantifiable benchmarks to assess progress, measuring Drury against its competitors. To match the scores of entering students at other institutions belonging to the Association of New American Colleges, the plan called for raising the ACT scores of Drury's entering class from an average of 25.5 to the 26–27 range.

The minimum objective was for Drury to continue to hold its own with these institutions, or better yet to surpass them. At the same time Drury would continue to maintain its Best Buy ranking, while shifting emphasis to compete with regional private schools instead of Missouri state schools. In addition to the 1,800 students in the day school, it set a goal of 3,500 for enrollment in the evening college, which at the time the plan was established stood at 2,500. This rate of growth for Continuing Studies was comparable to that which it had experienced over the previous ten years. The number of graduate students is targeted at 700, slightly more than double the number for 1999.

The plan shot for a target of 88 percent in freshman-to-sophomore retention and set a six-year graduation rate of 70 percent. In his memo to the faculty on February 13, 2004, Moore suggested that a "stretch rate might be 75 percent." Finally, the plan advocated raising the endowment to $250 million, a goal called "ambitious but achievable."

Throughout the summer of 2004, discussion sessions were held among trustees, staff, and faculty of Drury University. The meetings resulted in a list of Drury's key strengths and values over the past two decades to use as a guide for managing future growth and development. Among those strengths: small class size; a unique sense of community; excellence in teaching, including cooperation across academic disciplines; student-centeredness; athletic tradition; and international travel and study. Future goals included expanding program offerings, increasing academic rigor and standards, clarifying the relationship between day and evening school, and marketing Drury more effectively. Trustee Virginia Bussey expressed concern that the plan was too ambitious, and wondered whether Drury could keep its tuition hikes minimal while simultaneously trying to move to the next tier of liberal arts schools.

Increasing the student body by at least one-fifth will help appreciably but not in itself solve the problem, in the author's judgment. Moreover, there are limits as to how much the school's endowment can be tapped even if it doubles. Significantly raising alumni contributions via direct donations, estate gifts, and underwriting building and faculty endowments no doubt would help considerably. But the quickest and best way to improve revenues remains substantial tuition hikes that bring Drury's rates to the level of the institutions it wishes to emulate—assuredly a risky proposition. And while no single tactic is a panacea, *concomitant successes* will yield high cumulative dividends.

Speculative comments are no more than educated guesses. At the time this writing ended, the Drury story showed every sign of continuing to be an inspirational tale with a happy ending. The school's history is replete with dire prognostications about its future, all of which turned out to be way off the mark. During the Moore years, Drury had done so many things right and achieved so many remarkable results. Given that cumulative track record, there was every reason to be optimistic that when *The Drury Story III* appears twenty-five years from now, it will continue to hearten the reader with stories of the little school "that could and did."

# Epilogue

*There's a New Man in Town*

When John Moore announced his plan to retire at the end of the 2004–2005 academic year, a search committee consisting of nine trustees, three faculty, and two students was convened on October 29, 2004. From an initial pool of eighty candidates, the list was narrowed to eleven, all of whom underwent extensive off-campus interviews. Six semifinalists emerged to face a second round of interrogations from which the presidential search committee selected three finalists to visit the campus. On May 13, 2006, the Board of Trustees announced their selection of John Sellars to serve as Drury's fifteenth president, starting on June 1.

John Sellars has his roots in the Ozarks by way of Mountain View, Missouri, where the happy childhood he fondly recalls included visits to his grandfather's farm in Mountain Grove and float trips down the Jack's Fork River in nearby Eminence. Two of his three children and six of his seven grandchildren still live in the Show-Me State. The desire (shared with his wife Bette) to be closer to family played a part in his decision to apply for the presidency of Drury. But the most important reason for coming home, said Sellars, was because there was nothing better than "to go back to your roots where your family is from and be able to make a difference" (*Springfield News-Leader*, May 17, 2005). Sellars links his urge to make that productive difference to those childhood experiences in the Ozarks, where he encountered many people who did not have a lot of economic opportunities.

Volunteerism was a tradition in the Sellars family. His parents led groups of Boy Scouts and Girl Scouts. Young John sold potato chips door-to-door for the Boy Scouts; as an adult he served as a consultant to the Boy Scouts of America.

After graduating from Central Missouri State, where he earned a Bachelor of Science degree in Business Administration—he is also a CPA—Sellars went to work for Butler Manufacturing, serving first as plant comptroller and later as chief financial officer. Despite his success at the job, Sellars felt that "while I was in the business world, I always knew something was missing" (*Springfield News-Leader*, February 6, 2005). He pursued graduate studies at St. Paul's School of Theology in Minnesota while working as regional development and finance officer for the Community of Christ Church, and also earned a master's in public administration at the University of Missouri–Kansas City. That led to nine years at Graceland University in Lamoni, Iowa, where he held the titles of vice president for institution advancement and associate professor of business, while also obtaining a Ph.D. in education from the University of Missouri-Kansas City, where his thesis explored the elements that contribute to the success of small colleges and universities. Later, as senior vice president for advancement and marketing at Michigan Technological University, he was instrumental in helping to expand annual fund giving from $5 million to a high of $48 million. His success grew further during four years at Syracuse University, where as vice president for institutional advancement he increased gifts to the university from $45 million to $83 million.

Clearly then, Drury's new president brought to the table a wide variety of experiences, both inside and outside of academe. A proven track record in fund-raising, a consultative leadership style, and the willingness to make decisions contributed to the faculty's warm response to the announcement that Sellars would take the helm, beginning with a five-year contract (*Springfield News-Leader*, February 6, 2005; May 14, 2005). Search committee chairman John Beuerlein praised the strong fund-raising and management skills Sellars brought to Drury, noting, however, that "what impressed the committee even more was his scholarly research on the success of private universities, combined with a track record as a successful leader who sets ambitious goals and meets them."

In his inaugural address on October 28, 2005, President Sellars observed that Drury University attracted him because he knew it was a caring place embracing a culture of collegiality, outstanding faculty and staff, and dedicated alumni and friends. He stressed the importance of Drury's past history, emphasizing the continuity of its founders' goals of a college based on strong convictions, ethical behavior, and academic excellence, whose doors were open to all political and religious perspectives, and to men and women of all races.

His address also outlined his broad vision for Drury's future. It focused on making Drury a top university, whose graduates would become leaders in a global community. His plan for achieving these goals included these points: 1) Attract and retain the very best students and faculty, 2) Maintain a rich student services program geared to promoting opportunities for personal growth and leadership, 3) Provide facilities that enhance the Drury Experience, and 4) Increase financial resources to build an endowment commensurate with Drury's reputation.

Sellars' first year combined two missions: getting to know the Drury community, and beginning to set the stage for the university's leap forward. In meetings large and small, many at the President's House (redecorated by Bette, an artist, professor, and interior designer), he listened to faculty, staff, students, and alumni about their experience with Drury as it is, was, and could be.

From these conversations and his analysis of the university's operations, several themes emerged. The broadest was sustainability: practices that preserve the environment, as well as the health and dignity of its inhabitants. Keying on a student- and faculty-led dialogue connected to the 2005–2006 Theme Year, Sellars formed the President's Council on Sustainability, with the mission to help formulate policies and procedures to promote recycling, natural resource management and conservation, sustainable practices in facility renovation and construction, and ways to catalyze change on the campus and in the community. Biology Professors Don Deeds and Wendy Anderson were appointed cochairs of the council.

As noted earlier, the Drury chapter of SIFE, an international organization promoting entrepreneurship through community service and education, has received national and international recognition. Its award-winning activities offer the possibilities for a variety of entrepreneurial projects tied to campuswide themes. To tap that potential, President Sellars set up a Blue Ribbon Task Force. Its vision will see the light of day thanks to a $500,000 gift from financial services firm Edward Jones, and $1.5 million from Edward Jones general partner and Board of Trustees chair John Beuerlein and his wife, Crystal, to establish the Edward Jones Center for Entrepreneurship and Innovation, as reported in November 2006.

In step with these new initiatives, Sellars also directed his staff to begin planning for what is expected to be the largest fund-raising campaign in the university's history. The campaign will be driven by the needs for scholarships, academic and student life programming, and facilities as expressed by faculty, staff, and students across the campus.

As they implemented a new accounting and financial management system, Sellars and his cabinet also tackled an unexpected imbalance in operating funds caused by overspending on some of the university's recent capital projects. While the situation caused some anxiety on the campus, most—including those with the deepest knowledge of the numbers—believe it to be, as President Sellars has noted, "a bump in the road." The university's overall budget remained firmly in the black, and auditors, analysts, and trustees expressed confidence that the financial future of Drury was secure.

The goal of President Sellars' first year was to place Drury on its strongest footing yet, with a focused understanding at all levels of what makes Drury unique and successful, then to collaboratively envision the trajectory that will take Drury to new heights. Drury's future, while uncertain as it always is in times of change, is likely to be bright.

# Index

## A

ABC, 35, 148
Academy of Missouri Squires, 68
Adult Education Division, 96
Agruso, Victor, 49, 50, 52, 132
Air Force, 114
Alexander, Jerry, 110
Alger, Horatio, 130
Allen, Betty, 140
Allen, Calvin, 127
Allen, Charles, 124, 125
Allen, Jeanie, 94, 131, 132
Allen, Joan, 13
Allen, L. L., 23
Allen, Sandra, 139
Allies, 107, 120
Allison, Sean, 113
Alpha Lambda Delta, 107
Alpha Sigma Pi, 103
alumni, 12, 14, 29, 33, 36, 41, 46, 64, 69, 89, 99, 103, 136, 137, 153, 156, 162, 164, 165, 168, 170, 172, 173
Alumni Association, 33, 136, 137
Alumni Connections, 137
Alumni Council, 52, 82, 136
alumni couples, 84
Alumni Office, 156
Alumni Reunion, 23
Alumni Support, 164
America Writes for Kids, 126
American Advertising Federation, 126
American Association of University Professors, 44
American Chemical Society, 124
American College Test (ACT), 43
American Heart Association, 69
American Institute for Foreign Study, 93
American National Fish and Wildlife Museum, 68
American Society of Composers, Authors and Publishers (ASCAP), 126
Ameye, Don, 73
Anderson, Wendy, 125, 173
*Animal House*, 105
Armstrong, Judith, 132
Army, 63, 83, 96, 130
Articles of Association, 17, 24, 25
Asher, Ben, 14
Asher, Harvey, 9, 10, 132, 138
Asher, Sandy, 14, 126, 138
Ashley, George, 26
Associated New American Colleges (ANAC), 63, 73, 98
Associated Press, 60
Association of American Colleges and Universities, 85
*Association of American Colleges and Universities News*, 90
Association of Internet Researchers, 126
Association of Minority Minds, 107
Atha Pool, 34, 51, 146
Aurora, 60, 157
Ava, 97
Avery, Annette, 50, 51
Ayre, Rick, 36

175

## B

Bahn, Lorene, 133
Bailey, Eric, 110, 111
Baker, Dan, 51
Baker, Vivian, 140
Bamberger, Ruth, 125, 132
Barber Fitness Center, 146
Barber, Sharon and Butch, 146
Barnard, Tyler, 93
Bartholomy, John M., 13, 36, 39, 40, 41, 42, 43, 45, 46, 47, 48, 49, 54, 160
Barton, Thomas, 43
Bass, Shaun, 110
Bates, Stephanie, 114
Beach, Dan, 125
Beck, Eleanor, 132, 133
Bell, Harold, 130
Bell, Tanesha, 119
Belle Hall, 34, 125
Belushi, John, 105
Benne, Darrell, 37
Berger, William, 133
Beuerlein, Crystal, 173
Beuerlein, John, 13, 121, 153, 154, 159, 172, 173
Big Brothers/Big Sisters of the Ozarks, 94
Biosphere 2, 93
Black United Independent Colleges, 118
Blackwell, Macie, 139, 140
Blunt, Roy, 126
Board of Trustees, 11, 14, 24, 25, 28, 31, 36, 43, 48, 49, 52, 60, 64, 69, 72, 73, 120, 137, 145, 153, 159, 171, 173
Bonacker, Joyce, 133
Bond, Lora, 133, 154
Bone, James, 110
*Bonfire*, 107
Bothwell, Wilber E., 34, 96, 132
Boustani, Amine, 113
Boutwell, Gale, 13, 14, 135, 139
Boy Scouts of America, 107, 171
Boyd Elementary School, 96
Boyer, Ernest, 73
Boys and Girls Town, 94
Brandenburg, Earnest, 35
Breech Building, 34
Breech Pool, 146
Breech School of Business Administration, 95
Breech, Robert, 14, 58, 60, 145
Breedlove, Kasey, 96

Brierton, Pat, 13
Broaddus, Loren, 13, 57, 58, 60, 167
Browning, Carol, 124
Browning, Peter, 13, 17, 27
Brunson, Esther, 140
Buchholz, Jim, 13, 23, 62, 138, 143, 167
Buchholz, Marilyn, 14
Buckner, Mindy, 82
Burge School of Nursing, 34
Burnham Hall, 11, 31, 52, 64, 151
Burton, David, 15, 155
Bussey, Virginia, 13, 70, 169
Bynum, Jay, 52, 132

## C

Cabool, 97
Callen, Bruce, 125, 161
Campbell, Audrey, 84
Campus Exchange (CX), 46
Canon, Alfred O., 35, 36
Carbon Copy, 142
Cardenas, Nohora, 83
Carnegie Foundation, 31, 73, 117
Carnegie Mellon University, 147
Carnegie, Andrew, 21
Carney, Paul, 162, 165
Cascairo, Mark, 43
Cashel, Dan, 13, 110, 115
Center for Gifted Education, 151
Central High School, 125, 140
Chicago, Judy, 88
Chipperfield, Lynn, 36
Churchill, Gladys, 139, 140
Churchill, Rhonda, 107
Civil Rights Movement, 36, 42, 117
Civil War, 14, 18, 19, 21, 22, 27
Clara Thompson Hall, 15, 32, 46, 60, 75, 154
Claussen, Jackie, 140
Clayton, Penny, 14
Clinton, Peggy, 82
Clippinger, Frank, 9, 10, 14, 35
College Democrats, 106
College Park, 66, 102, 103, 105, 132, 136, 157
Colorado College, 159
Columbia College, 18
Columbia University, 93
Comer Project, 96, 168
Common Cause, 125
Compas, Krystal, 13, 161, 162, 165
Congregationalist Church, 23
Connecticut College, 159

Continuing Education Division, 41, 50, 97, 126
Cooley, Emma, 30
Cooper, Lisa, 14
Council of Independent Colleges, 73, 78, 89
Coursin, Edith, 140
Covington, Louise, 133
Cowherd, Barb, 13, 141
Cox, Bob, 64
Cox, Claudine, 57
Cox, Lester, 34, 152
Cox, Robert, 13
Cox-Bussey, Virginia, 152
Crawford, Norman C., 11, 13, 15, 47, 48, 49, 50, 51, 52, 53, 54, 57, 71, 146, 160
Creech, Ormal, 57
CX, 46, 139, 140, 141, 142

# D

*Dark of the Moon*, 41
Davies, Tristan, 6, 13
Dead White Males, 42, 117
DeBerry, Charlie, 71
Deeds, Don, 13, 14, 70, 74, 84, 124, 152, 173
Dees, Morris, 88
Deffebaugh, Tommy, 110
Delta Delta Delta, 106
Democratic National Convention, 117
Denton, Rebecca, 119
Department of Education, 125
Development and Alumni Relations, 104, 150
Dill, Darlene, 13, 137
Disciples of Christ, 23, 119, 136
Disciples on Campus, 107
Discovery Center of Springfield, 149
Distinguished Alumni Awards, 137
Diversity Center, 65, 119, 120
Dixon, Bob, 66, 105
Donald and Ruth Martin Alumni Center, 104
Drury, 9, 10, 11, 12, 13, 14, 17, 19, 22, 24, 25, 26, 27, 28, 29, 30, 31, 32, 33, 34, 35, 36, 37, 39, 40, 41, 42, 43, 44, 45, 46, 47, 48, 49, 50, 51, 52, 53, 54, 55, 56, 57, 60, 61, 62, 63, 64, 65, 66, 67, 69, 70, 71, 72, 73, 74, 75, 76, 77, 78, 79, 81, 82, 83, 84, 86, 87, 88, 89, 90, 91, 92, 93, 94, 95, 96, 97, 98, 99, 101, 102, 103, 104, 105, 106, 107, 108, 110,
111, 112, 113, 114, 115, 116, 117, 118, 119, 120, 121, 122, 123, 124, 125, 126, 127, 128, 129, 130, 131, 132, 133, 135, 136, 137, 138, 139, 140, 141, 142, 143, 145, 146, 147, 148, 149, 150, 151, 153, 154, 155, 156, 157, 159, 160, 162, 163, 164, 165, 167, 168, 169, 170, 171, 172, 173, 174
Drury Ambassadors, 137
Drury Center, 93
Drury Choir, 41
Drury Cinema Club, 107
Drury College, 13, 17, 18, 21, 23, 24, 43, 45, 50, 74, 96, 145, 160
Drury Concert Band, 75
Drury Conservatory, 155
Drury Diversity Center, 65
Drury Friends Program, 83
Drury Interfraternity Council (IFC), 103
Drury Jazz Band, 75
Drury Jazz Swingers, 37
*Drury Lane*, 14, 18, 23, 30, 34, 36, 78, 82, 118, 150, 151
*Drury Mirror*, 14, 30, 51, 52, 60, 63, 66, 103
Drury Orchestra, 75
Drury Plan, 33, 42
*Drury Quarterly*, 14, 36, 107, 130
Drury Singers, 37, 75, 107
Drury University, 6, 9, 11, 73, 85, 111, 116, 147, 159
Drury University's Core Curriculum, 90
Drury Woodwind Quintet, 75
Drury, Albert, 24
Drury, Samuel, 24
Drury-Evangel Orchestra, 41
Dukert, Betty Cole, 14
DUTV, 107, 147

# E

East Academy Building, 29
Eaton, Randy, 82
Edward Jones, 154, 173
Edward Jones Center for Entrepreneurship and Innovation, 173
Ehrenreich, Barbara, 88
Eikner, Allen, 42, 132
Elliot, Brenda, 13
endowment, 27, 32, 33, 42, 43, 156, 162, 163, 169, 170, 173
Environmental Club, 107, 118

Eriksson, Per, 113
Esposito, Lisa, 13, 74
Ess, Charlie, 126
Everheart, William, 12, 36
Exercise and Sports Science Department, 146
experimental learning, 102
*Extreme Makeover—Home Edition*, 148

## F

Facilities Services, 142, 143, 144
Fairbanks Hall, 29, 34, 39
Fairbanks, Charles, 29
Family Violence Center, 94
Federal Medical Center, 68
Feiler, Bruce, 88
Fellowship of Christian Athletes, 107
Findlay Student Center, 36, 52, 60, 113, 143, 144, 152, 155
Findlay, James L., 33, 34, 35, 64
First-Year Experience, 84, 94, 131
Fisk College, 18
Flanangan, Price, 15
Flikkema, Eltjen, 13, 45, 50, 51, 91, 118
Foltz, Allen, 132
For the Common Good, 88, 126
Fort Leonard Wood, 96, 97, 157
Foster, Kelly, 76
Freeman Hall, 151
Freeman, Falvius and Frances, 151
Freeman-Smith, Mercedes, 151
French, Kevin, 138
French, Valerie, 138
Fryer, Oscar, 12, 83, 133, 141, 154
Fulbright, 124, 126
Fuller, Randy, 91, 126

## G

Gadd, Cecilia, 113
Garrott, Jay, 13, 15, 147
Garvin, Bill, 13, 18, 30
Geiger, Roger, 14
Gettysburg College, 159
Global Perspectives 21 (GP21), 72, 82, 85, 86, 87, 131
Gohn, David, 69
Good, Judy, 14, 77
Good, Steve H., 13, 14, 49, 53, 55, 62, 70, 71, 72, 73, 74, 75, 76, 77, 78, 79, 85, 86, 88, 91, 122, 133, 136, 139, 147, 152, 160

Goza, David, 76
Graduate and Continuing Studies, 86, 97
Graduate Education Program, 96
Graves, Willard, 133
Great Awakening, 19, 21
Great Depression, 33
Great Lakes Valley Conference (GLVC), 116
Great Lakes Valley Western Division, 112
Greater Ozarks Business Hall of Fame, 69
Greene County Financial Advisory Board, 68
Greene, Brian, 88
Griffin, James, 132
Grigg, Anna, 25
Grimm, Leigh, 14
Grimm, Wally, 13, 14, 64
Guillebeau, Julie, 49

## H

Habitat for Humanity, 107, 149
Hales, Harrison, 27
Hall, James, 75
Hammerstein, Oscar, 35
Hammons Corporation, 148
Hammons, John, 69, 147
Hankansson, Lourette, 113
Harding, Bill, 57, 115, 132
Harger, Bruce, 111, 112, 114, 115, 133
Harrison Stadium, 67, 68
Harwood Hall, 147
Harwood Library, 32
Harwood, Charles E., 23
Harwood, James H., 23, 24, 28
Haseltine, Art, 136
Heartland Conference, 108, 111, 113, 115, 116
Hem Sheela Model School, 125
Henson, Kristi, 128
Hesser, Steve, 111, 112
Hill, Ed, 132
Himmelreich, Howard, 133
Hinrichs, Brant, 107
*History Reborn*, 66
Hlatshwayo, Matifazda, 119
Hoblit Room, 151
Hoblit, Marian, 151
Hoeman, Michael, 68
Hoff-Summers, Christina, 88
Hogarth, Thomas, 76
Holdren, Karolyn, 13, 139, 141

Holmes, D. Wayne, 15, 70, 71, 129, 130, 131, 132
Holmes, Lonnie, 110
Holmes-Folkes, Robin, 155
Holstrum, John, 13
Honors Program, 91, 92, 168
Hope, Bob, 36
Hopkins, Paula, 13
Horton, Bob, 66
House of Representatives, 125
Howatt, Gordon H., 51
Hudson, Peter, 119
Hudson, Terry, 133
Hughes, Marsha, 97
Hulston, John, 57
Hutchens Health, Physical Education, and Recreation Facility (HPER), 145

## I

Ingalls, Francis T., 29
Ingersol, Robert, 133
Ingraham, Jennifer, 96
Institute for Experiential Learning, 94
Institute for Mature Learners, 99
Interdisciplinary Studies Center, 90
International Student Association (ISA), 83, 107, 120
*Introduction to Economic Reasoning*, 126
Iran, 42
Ireland, 88

## J

Jackson, Rosemary, 132
Jakeman, Rick, 94
Jefferson Park, 103
Jefferson, Thomas, 86
Jiracek, Jakub, 113
John Q. Hammons School of Architecture, 15, 147, 148, 149
Johnson, Ken, 99
Johnson, Wayne, 133
Jones, Aaron, 13
Jones, Adelaide, 96
Jones, Carol, 127
Jones, John, 155
Joseph, Don Verne, 37
Judeo-Christian tradition, 87

## K

Kahut, Jodie, 43

Kappa Alpha, 22, 31, 67, 103, 104, 105, 106
Kappa Delta, 96, 106
Kappa Mu Epsilon, 106
KDRU, 107, 147
Kellogg, Tom, 56
Kellogg's Corn Flakes, 95
Kent State, 36
Kenton, Stan, 37
Killough, Richard, 93, 132
King, Martin Luther, 119
Kirby, Susan, 13, 136, 137, 141
Kirtlink, Jennifer, 139
Klingner, Mary Elizabeth, 133
Koehler, Steve, 64, 66
Krassner, Avice, 140
Kresge Foundation, 154
KTTS, 51
KULR, 41, 52
Kunstler, William, 37

## L

Lambda Chi Alpha, 103, 104, 106
Lancaster Museum of Art, 126
Landsdowne College, 93
Langford, Michelle, 113
Lay Hall, 61, 141, 152, 154
Lay Science Center, 35, 152
Lebanon, 96, 97, 157
Lee, J. Scott, 90
Lewis, Mike, 113
Library Plaza, 151
Living Learning Communities (LLCs), 92, 102, 132, 136
Livingston, James, 132
Logos, 107
Lombardi, Vince, 116
Long, Kevin, 13, 142, 143
Loughrige, Craig, 127
Lucas, C. J., 14
*Luge*, 126
Lumina Foundation, 125
Lüneburg University, 93
Luttrell, Vickie, 13, 125, 132
Lydy Art Center, 46
Lydy Foundation, 43
Lydy Presidential Scholarships, 43
Lydy-O'Bannon Center, 45
Lynch, Tom, 136

## M

Mabee Foundation, 46, 154
Mack, Cashel, 113

Maddux, Mindy, 102
Maender, Chris, 113
Mahvi Educational Foundation, 42
Make-A-Wish Foundation, 68
Mallory, Arthur, 57
Manley Hall, 103
Maritime Commission, 34
*Mark and Livy—The Love Story of Mark Twain and the Woman Who Almost Tamed Him* (1994), 126
Martin, Don, 14, 49
Martin, Judy, 46, 47, 48, 49, 52, 62, 70, 150, 156
Martin, Ruth, 14
mascot, 30, 115
Matthew, Craig, 84
Matthews, Edsel, 111, 115, 116
Matthews, Sherrie, 13
Matusevich, Maxim, 13, 107, 122
Maxson, Rick, 92
McAdoo, Joe, 92, 127, 132
McAlear, Tom, 14
McCabe Foundation, 125
McConnell, Randy, 36
McCullagh Cottage, 34, 35
McGowan, Paul, 84
McKinney, Anton, 118
Meador, Lewis E., 35, 36
Mears, Harriet, 132
Mears, Richard, 132, 133
Medico, Ann, 115
Mercer, Charles, 42, 133
Middlebury College, 14
Mideast oil embargo, 46
Midtown Neighborhood Association, 66
Midwest Model United Nations, 106
Milas, Lawrence J., 149, 150
Miller, John, 13, 143, 144, 159
Miller, Matt, 110
Miller, Rebecca, 126
Miller, Robin, 126
Milleson, Nyla, 112
Minasian, Sam, 132
Minton, Steve, 148
Missouri Association for College Admissions Counseling (MOACAC), 83
Missouri Colleges Fund, 68
Missouri Geographic Alliance, 125
Monroe, Ruth, 13, 14, 125, 140
Montclair Retirement Home, 106
Mooberry, Philip, 110
Moody, Rick, 88
Moore, Bruce, 149
Moore, John E., 10, 11, 13, 14, 55, 56, 57, 60, 61, 62, 63, 64, 65, 66, 67, 68, 69, 70, 72, 73, 77, 79, 83, 88, 105, 111, 122, 135, 145, 147, 149, 150, 151, 152, 153, 154, 159, 160, 162, 163, 164, 165, 168, 169, 170, 171
Morris, John L., 104
Morrison, Nathan J., 18, 23, 24, 25, 26, 27, 28, 29, 30
Mortar Board, 30, 107
Mortellaro, Chris, 110
Moser, Patrick, 125
Mullins, Steve, 69
Murrow, James, 13, 126, 127, 139

# N

Nadal, Thomas W., 31, 32, 33
Naeger, Stacey, 13
National Academic Advising Association, 126
National Architecture Accrediting Board (NAAB), 147
National Association of Biology Teachers, 125
National Association of Intercollegiate Athletics (NAIA), 45
National Collegiate Athletic Association (NCAA), 108
National Endowment for the Arts, 124
National Endowment of the Humanities, 126
National Guard, 36
National Institutes of Health, 125
National Labor Relations Board (NLRB), 45
National Science Foundation (NSF), 89, 124
National Survey of Student Engagement, 85
Nelms, Ann, 137
Nelson, Jennifer, 84
Newbold, Andrea, 106
Newton, Amanda, 108, 109
Nickle, Ted, 132
Nixon, Richard, 117
Norris, Joye, 98, 99
North Atlantic Treaty Organization (NATO), 114
North Central Association (NCA), 53, 72, 98, 168
Northwest Missouri State University, 111

Nowak, Paul, 126, 127

## O

O'Bannon Music Center, 46
O'Bannon, Dorothy, 46
O'Bannon, George, 46
O'Reilly, David, 104
O'Reilly, Larry, 104
O'Reilly-Morris House, 104
oil embargo, 46
Olin Library, 75, 126, 143, 148, 150, 156
Oliver, Brad, 115
Olivet College, 23, 24, 32
Omicron Delta Kappa, 107
Operation Overlord, 93
Overstreet, Sarah, 105
Ozark Council of Churches, 68
Ozarks, 35, 57, 63, 68, 69, 78, 89, 94, 97, 99, 106, 110, 115, 130, 131, 157, 171

## P

Padron, Dorothy, 14
Padron, Jorge, 36, 41, 42, 46, 47, 49, 50, 132, 154
Page, Phil, 41
Panhellenic Hall, 156
Pantoja, Rodrigo, 83
Panza, Chris, 74
Parker, Chip, 13, 82
Parker, Jane, 14, 69
Parker, Tom, 76, 155
Parnell, Ben, 69
Parnell, Todd, 14
Parsonage, 157
Pastar, Marin, 83
Pearl Harbor, 34
Pearsons Hall, 31, 83, 143, 151
Peel, Marcus, 110
Peeples, David, 43
Penny, Patti, 127
Perischetti, Vincent, 76
*Peter and the Wolf*, 94
Peter Hudson Ethnic Diversity Scholarship, 119
Petty, Cliff, 13, 128
Phi Alpha Theta, 106
Phi Beta Kappa, 22
Phi Kappa Sigma, 103
Pi Beta Phi, 31, 106
Pipkin Junior High, 68

Policy Center on the First Year of College, 84
Pool Art Center, 126, 155
Pool, Barbara Spencer, 155
Pool, Earl, 155
Pool, Mary Jane, 13, 14, 57, 59, 155
Posey, Tim, 13
Pre-Health Club, 107
Prejean, Helen, 88
Preparatory School, 19, 20, 28, 29
Prevent Child Abuse America, 96
Price-Waterhouse, 33
*Princeton Review*, 81
Project Kaleidoscope (PKAL), 88
Prokoviev, Sergei, 94
Puryear, Scott, 115
Pyle, Bill, 14
Pyle, Joyce, 14, 83

## Q

Quinn, Nathaniel, 110

## R

Radecki, Pete, 13, 163
Rader, Gary, 98
Radio Shack's World Cup, 95
Red Cross, 34, 106
Reed College, 159
Reed, Lyle, 13, 63, 153
Regents College, 93
Reichert, Bev, 98
Reid, Florence, 140
retention rate, 166
Reynolds, Brian, 113
Richardson, Katy, 83
Richardson, Kevin, 141
Richmond, Red, 13, 143
Riley, James, 44, 46, 132
Roach, Bob, 14
Robb, Larry F., 14
Rodgers, Richard, 35
Roe, Tiffany, 13
Rogers, Tyler, 111
Rohlf, Bill, 126, 128
Rolla, 97, 157
Rollins, Sue, 97, 98
Ronald McDonald House, 94
Rotary Club, 68, 127, 128
Roulet, Paul, 26
Rowell, Lee, 39
Roy, Protima, 14, 125
Roy, Rabindranath, 13, 125
Russo, Tom, 155

Rutan, Steve, 132

## S

Sacks, Oliver, 88
San Paolo, Ann, 138
Sanders, Melody, 13
Sarkodee-Adoo, Jody, 149
Schie, Ron, 126
Schlosser, Eric, 88
Schmidt, George P., 14
School of the Ozarks, 35, 110
Schraft, Rob, 13
Schreiner, Pat, 13, 78
Schroer, Susie, 75
Schur, Richard, 90, 126
Sears Director's Cup, 116
Sellars, Bette, 171, 173
Sellars, John D., 13, 158, 159, 160, 161, 163, 171, 172, 173, 174
Seven Sages Society, 32
Shaffer, Georgia, 138
Sharpe, Carlyle, 126
Shepard, Edward M., 27, 28
*Shepherd of the Hills*, 130
Shewmaker Communication Center, 146, 147, 157
Shewmaker, Jack, 147
Shewmaker, Melba, 147
Shewmaker, Shari, 147
Shrine Mosque, 60
Siebert, Scotti, 13, 141
Sigma Nu, 103, 104, 106
Sigma Phi, 22
Simmons, Dale, 75
Simmons, John, 53, 147
Skinner, Stanley, 155
Smal-Mart, 102
Smith Hall, 101
Smith, James, 49, 132
Smith, Sam, 132
Sooter, Tracy, 13
Southeastern Psychological Association, 124
Southwest Missouri State University, 39, 97, 113, 125
Southwest Teachers Credit Union, 67
Spencer Cottage, 29
Spires, Erica, 76
sports, 12, 78, 108, 110, 112, 115, 127, 130
Sports Information Office, 14
Sprenger, Robin, 13, 130
Springer, Wallace, 53, 59, 60
Springfield, 22, 23, 24, 25, 41, 43, 46, 48, 49, 51, 60, 65, 67, 69, 82, 83, 92, 94, 96, 97, 99, 101, 106, 107, 110, 112, 120, 125, 126, 129, 146, 149, 157, 165, 167
Springfield Art Museum, 92
Springfield Association of Congregational Churches, 23
Springfield Chamber of Commerce, 68, 129
Springfield College, 17, 24
Springfield Contractors Association, 69
Springfield Hall, 142
*Springfield Leader and Press*, 41, 46, 48, 51
*Springfield News-Leader*, 14, 105, 110, 111, 127, 131, 171, 172
Springfield Public Schools, 67, 96
Springfield School District, 67
SS *Drury Victory*, 34
St. John's Hospital, 126
St. Jude's Cancer Research Hospital, 106
Staab, Ron, 113
Stahl, Richard, 101
Stameshkin, David, 14
Stanfield, Gary, 110, 111
Stanfield, Sandy, 110
Starczewski, Jerzy, 132
Stauffer, Larry, 132
Steck, Jack, 51, 113
Still, Kelly, 126
Stillwell, Carl, 35
Stoan, Steve, 126
Stocker, Jenelle, 94
Stockton, 157
Stone Chapel, 28, 35, 36, 60, 135, 151, 154
Stone, Valerie, 18, 27, 28
Stratton, Mark, 115
Stratton, Sara, 112
Strube, W. Curtis, 14, 127, 128, 129, 133
Student Alumni Association, 107
Student Senate, 32, 37, 41, 51, 52
Student Union Board, 37, 41, 52, 106
Students in Free Enterprise (SIFE), 95, 103, 119
Sullivan, Dan, 113
Summer Quest, 67
Summerscape, 67
Summit Park, 94, 101, 102
Summit Place, 94
Sunderland Hall, 34, 101, 102, 144, 157
Susan G. Komen Breast Cancer Foundation, 106

Swearengin, Kim, 113
Sweeney, Karen, 13, 50, 52, 53, 60, 61, 62, 104, 105, 135, 136, 160, 161, 162
Swinburne University, 93

## T

Taking a Stand for Kids, 94
Tate, Maurice, 65, 66
Taylor, Charles, 95, 160
Taylor, John, 125
Terry, Sean, 125
Tewsbury, Donald, 14
Thayer, 97, 157
*The Haunting of American Literature—Emerson and the Critical Imagination*, 126
The Team, 115
Theme Year Convocation series, 88
Thomas Edison College, 53
Thomas, Darcy, 93
Thomas, Dean, 155
Thomas, Jim, 148
Thomas, Michael, 61
Thomas, Reagan, 107
Thwing, Charles, 14
Tillman, Charles, 41
*Time* magazine, 84
Toby the Skeleton, 154
*Today* show, 95
Torpey, Sarah, 93
Trends in Liberal Arts Project, 90
Trustee Science Center, 70, 150, 152, 153, 154, 156
Tsinghua University, 93
Turner Hall, 34, 143

## U

*U.S. News and World Report*, 81, 167
United Sports Academy, 116
United States Maritime Commission, 34
United Way of the Ozarks, 68
University Communications Office, 14
University of Copenhagen, 93
University of Granada, 93
Unwind Grind, 155
Upper White River Basin Foundation, 68
*Upstart Crow*, 130
*USA Today*, 116

## V

VanDenBerg, Jeff, 14, 78
Venture Crew, 107
Vietnam War, 35, 36, 42, 117
Vise, Ilga, 98, 142
Vise, Sidney, 78, 132, 155

## W

Walker Hall, 151
Walker Library, 34, 60, 149
Walker, Marvin, 110, 115, 140
Wallace Hall, 32, 34, 101
Washington Avenue Baptist Church, 65
Washington Avenue Baptist Youth Dance Troupe, 119
Washington Center, 94
Wasson, Bill, 14, 141
Waters, Regina, 75, 126
Watts, Parris, 99
Weaver Elementary School, 94
Webb, Ben, 147
Weber, Don, 142
Weddle, Rob, 13
Weddle, Sandra, 126
Weiser Gymnasium, 33, 46, 109, 110, 111, 112, 113, 143, 145
Weiser, Albert, 33
Wells, Chuck, 13, 167
West, Edythe, 82
West, Susan, 37, 82
White, A. J., 110
White, Jayne, 96
White, John Turner, 25
Wiles, Jennifer, 14, 48, 49, 50, 52
Wilhoit, Robert, 132
Willcox, Ella, 28
William & Mary College, 18
William Woods College, 46
Williams College, 23
Williams, Greg, 129
Williams, Ken, 66
Willis, Resa, 126
Wing, Barbara, 125, 154
Winter 2002 Olympic Festival Concerts, 126
Wood, Mark, 67, 125, 152
Woodland Cottage, 30
Woodwind Quintet, 75
World War I, 32
World War II, 34
Worley, Rusty, 13, 66, 67
Wyatt, Robert, 95

## Y

Yahoo! Internet Life, 81
Young Republicans, 106
Young, Brigham, 113
Young, Roger, 13, 74
Young, Ted, 110
Yount, Jim, 113

## Z

Zeta Tau Alpha, 31, 106
Zuhal, Nida, 113

www.ingramcontent.com/pod-product-compliance
Lightning Source LLC
Chambersburg PA
CBHW031956080426
42735CB00007B/409